5 Essential Skills for Successful School Leaders
Second Edition

Other Books by the Authors

Real Classroom Management: Whose Job Is It?
5 Essential Skills of School Leadership: Moving from Good to Great, First Edition

5 Essential Skills for Successful School Leaders
Second Edition

Moving from Good to Great

Nancy Langley and Mark M. Jacobs

ROWMAN & LITTLEFIELD
Lanham • Boulder • New York • London

Published by Rowman & Littlefield
4501 Forbes Boulevard, Suite 200, Lanham, Maryland 20706
www.rowman.com

16 Carlisle Street, London W1D 3BT, United Kingdom

Copyright © 2014 by Nancy Langely and Mark M. Jacobs

All rights reserved. No part of this book may be reproduced in any form or by any electronic or mechanical means, including information storage and retrieval systems, without written permission from the publisher, except by a reviewer who may quote passages in a review.

British Library Cataloguing in Publication Information Available

Library of Congress Cataloging-in-Publication Data

Langley, Nancy, 1952– .
5 essential skills for successful school leaders : moving from good to great / Nancy Langely and Mark M. Jacobs.
p. cm.
Includes bibliographical references.
ISBN 978-1-4758-1017-2 (cloth) -- ISBN 978-1-4758-1018-9 (pbk.) -- ISBN 978-1-4758-1019-6 (electronic)
1. Educational leadership. I. Jacobs, Mark M., 1947- II. Title. III. Title: Five essential skills for school leaders.
LB2831.6.L36 2014
371.2—dc23
2014009983

Contents

Preface	vii
Foreword	ix
1 Setting the Record Straight on Terminology	1
2 Leadership Styles	5
3 One Final Word Before We Present the Five Skills	11
4 The Ability to Be Insightful	17
5 Positive, Strong Interpersonal Skills	27
6 Self-Growth	31
7 Flexibility	39
8 Keeping in Touch with the Community	49
9 Bringing It All Together	55
10 Now What?	71
11 One Final Point	79
12 Your Turn	83
Bibliography	93
About the Authors	95

Preface

What is the definition of a leader? What makes a good leader a great leader? How do the events that contribute to our changing environment, as presented by local or national government, ultimately affect leadership styles and decisions? The aim of this book is to address these issues and present information that can help guide leaders in the field of education through routine—and perhaps some not-so-routine—situations.

Recently, we were examining the characteristics and/or traits of a good leader. While reviewing some cases of similar incidents that occurred in different school districts, we noticed that although the resolution of these issues should have been alike if not equal, some districts reached more favorable results than others. We came to the conclusion that the results varied because the leadership styles in each case were different. Neither size nor location of the districts or leaders had much of an impact on the outcome.

Therefore, we set out to research what the experts in the field had to offer as a definition of a successful leader. The product of our investigation was a survey that led to an article published in the *American School Board Journal* in September 2002. As a follow-up to the article, we decided that this topic was so interesting that we set out to share our findings via workshops, seminar presentations, and further writings and to seek continued input from our colleagues.

As you read the following pages, you will see a variety of examples of situations that you, as an educator, may encounter. At the end of the book you will find several exercises to help you develop a successful plan, should similar situations occur in your school or district. Personal experiences are, of course, the easiest to relate to others. Therefore, some of the examples we use in this book will refer to things we have experienced where we have worked. We also solicited information and real-life examples from our colleagues and friends from other districts around the country to include urban, suburban, and rural areas. The districts we targeted ranged in size from just under 9,000 students to just over 168,000 students.

The names of people and places are anonymous. We hope that as you read our words, you will relate the examples to your own surroundings as well as other districts you are familiar with through readings or friends or family.

Before we delve into this work, we would like to take a moment to express our heartfelt thanks to our friends and families who have had to make some adjustments to their lives so that we could find the time to work on our surveys, lectures, workshops, and writings. We would like to extend special thanks goes out to five people without whom we might not have even started our research. Those special people are Dave Pratt, Bill Mackenzie, Kenneth Gaudreault, Betsy Goodman, and Marty Abbott.

Foreword

The challenges of school leadership in the twenty-first century demand so much of the individuals willing to take on that challenge. Successful leaders are required to be visionary, technology savvy, analytical, and effective communicators among a long list of additional attributes. When students enter the Educational Leadership Program at St. John Fisher College, they have some experience in leadership roles either in their personal or professional lives and are confident they have what it takes. Shortly after they begin the program they learn there is so much about effective leadership for them to learn.

The first course in the program examines, in depth, the core values and characteristics of effective leadership and connecting leadership research with best practices. Since 2007 the *5 Essential Skills for Successful School Leaders: Moving from Good to Great* has been used as a text for this first course. Our faculty agrees with the authors' statement, "this book is only the first step in bringing you from the point of being a good leader to becoming a great leader," and we emphasize this statement with our students.

The construction of a building and a successful career requires providing a strong foundation. Our experience has been that the *5 Essential Skills for Successful School Leaders: Moving from Good to Great* provides a strong foundation for effective school leadership. The students are assigned to read the book, and each chapter is discussed in class. The discussions that take place are very lively, in part because students can relate to the descriptions of the leaders and scenarios, as a result of personal experiences or situations they have heard about.

As students move through the program, citations from the book are frequently used to support the positions taken in writing responses to case studies or other course requirements. The insights gained by students from this book also have informed their understanding of motivational theories, developing and sustaining effective partnerships with community stakeholders, effective instructional leadership, professional development, performance evaluations, and being a reflective practitioner (topics covered in future courses).

The implementation of the Common Core, increasing demands for quantifiable educator accountability, and the infusion of social media into the lives of our youth are all new challenges faced by twenty-first-century school leaders as they move through the second decade of this century. Effective school leaders must be prepared to address these and other issues; the *5 Essential Skills for Successful School Leaders: Moving from Good to Great* provides a solid foundation and helps to prepare future educational leaders to be effective, reflective practitioners striving to be great.

William B. Stroud, EdD
assistant professor, codirector
Educational Leadership Program
St. John Fisher College

Chapter One

Setting the Record Straight on Terminology

Who would read a book simply titled *5 Essential Skills for School Leaders*? There are scores of leadership books and articles proclaiming that if you follow their suggestions, you will become a successful leader, regardless of whether the leader is an educator or is part of the business world. No doubt, each one of these books is full of useful information and guidance. However, in this book, we are examining not only what makes a leader successful but also how to use your leadership skills in our ever-changing environment.

Working with the information in this book is only the first step in bringing you from the point of being a good leader to becoming a great leader. Making it all work and becoming a truly successful leader is up to you. Which paths you follow in life is something controlled by you and only you. You are the sole determining player who must decide what changes to make and how to approach your daily challenges.

We will focus for a moment on the title we have chosen. What makes this book so unique and essential is that we will discuss how the rapid pace of changes in our lives must be met and therefore work together to form the successful leader. The way you address the challenges you will encounter on a typical day will be the litmus test of your ability to effectively motivate your colleagues and reach your goals. The enjoyment gained from seeing these positive results will then prove to be motivating factors for the leader. Together, we will explore these everyday issues and discover how we should turn unpleasant challenges into pleasant and rewarding situations.

Leaders in today's world must make every attempt to adapt to change in a manner that incorporates specific skills, be they inherent or learned, to become successful. In other words, flexibility is a key factor in our lives—but we will discuss that in detail in an upcoming chapter. The most important thing to keep in mind is that the end goal of all our efforts is to provide our students the best academic and safest learning environment possible.

Finally, the accomplishments of a successful leader must not be looked on as an individual achievement but should be measured by the following:

- The overall improvement of our workplace, such as the good use of strong interpersonal skills, flexibility, and insightfulness—all of which we will address shortly.
- Meeting the needs of our clients, namely, the students—and having a good working relationship with parents and other members of the community.
- How well we continue to strive for success through self-growth—another very important goal.
- The level of student performance and activity in academics and overall involvement in schools.
- Highly qualified, professional teachers.

WHAT WE MEAN BY LEADER

When you look up the definition of leader, you will find descriptive words such as *guide* or *conductor*. We would like to take this a step further by stating that any time a person must make a decision that has an impact on another, he or she is by definition a leader. Therefore, any situation in which a person must make a decision that affects others identifies that person as a leader. Since it is almost impossible to make a decision that does not affect anyone other than the decision maker, we can then say that we are all leaders at one time or another.

Superintendents are leaders of groups and individuals from many levels, principals lead all who are associated with their individual schools, and classroom teachers directly lead their students and indirectly, through their accomplishments, serve to lead colleagues who emulate or are affected by their actions.

Students lead on the playground and in the classroom as peer mentors or whenever they engage in an extra risk-taking step to guide their group. They lead when they are the first to raise their hands to answer a question. No matter in which category of leadership we find ourselves, the goals we set should always be aimed at being a successful leader.

What qualities should we possess to be considered a successful leader? We posit that this is someone who understands, adopts, and demonstrates good use of five commonly shared qualities or characteristics, as outlined in this book. We should make an attempt to understand how the dynamics of individual peculiarity affects a person's ability to manage.

The key to success, therefore, is the person who is understanding, has keen foresight, is willing to be flexible, displays good interpersonal skills (including the ability to delegate), and constantly strives for continued personal and professional growth. There are five essential qualities that, when properly employed, will result in successful leadership. We will present each of these traits separately and in detail as five chapters titled "The Ability to Be Insightful," "Positive, Strong Interpersonal Skills," "Self-Growth," "Flexibility," and "Keeping in Touch with the Community." We will also demonstrate that while each character trait is essential and may, at times, stand alone, for the most part they will unavoidably overlap.

Additionally, each chapter will illustrate how the results of these traits are evidenced by higher productivity achieved in a positive educational environment. Once you establish the correlation between the priorities of the school or district and the leaders involved, you are ready to set a plan in motion. As leaders, it is our goal to bring our organizations to a higher level—to increase test scores, to provide safe and productive learning environments, to enhance the ability of our teachers, and to support the needs of the community.

Chapter Two

Leadership Styles

Before getting into the specifics, we should talk about leadership styles in general. There are, as one might imagine, almost as many different management styles as there are leaders. However, John Ivancevich and William Glueck (1983), in their book *Foundations of Personnel: Human Resource Management*, present two specific categories that they contend are the foundation stones of leadership styles: Theory X and Theory Y. A Theory X leader is a person who is the micromanager and who uses coercion and threats in order to motivate subordinates. In other words, someone who exercises this type of behavior can be called the authoritarian leader.

In the business world as well as the academic arena, there is an underworld of management styles, so to speak, that some senior power holders use to get results. Although at times the desired result is achieved, the end is not justified by the means. James T. Scarnati (2002), in an article titled "The Godfather Theory of Management: An Exercise in Power and Control," uses an analogy to Mario Puzo's Godfather series and the movie trilogy that followed. In this article, Scarnati points out that the motion picture "depicts a brutal organizational and management system based on power, control and manipulation" (p. 1).

Two of the three Corleone brothers had specific flaws that directly affected their ability to lead successfully. For example, Sonny Corleone, the privileged son, was slotted to become the new godfather. Unfortunately, his display of anger and rashness and his hot-temperedness brought him to meet his ultimate fate at a toll booth on the New Jersey Turnpike. Certainly we want to avoid following in his footsteps! We draw the comparison, however, to Sonny and the Theory X leader—to the extreme.

In the real world, we examined the case of a particular individual of a midsized firm in New York State who is the perfect example of the nonpreferred Theory X person. We will discuss later that there are, in fact, sometimes that Theory X qualities are acceptable. However, in this instance, the leader in question ruled with a very heavy hand and exercised actions that caused fear, anger, and much dissent among the employees.

Employees were afraid to go to work and equally reluctant to call in sick. Their home and family lives were affected. Their level of stress was elevated, often causing health-related problems. They complained among themselves—too afraid to approach their boss and sure that their remarks to him would produce undesirable results—and spent their time away from work seeking other employment. Meanwhile, their assignments were usually accomplished, but because of the unhappy atmosphere created on the site, the employees did not put their best effort into the task, resulting in shoddy work.

Another example of this type of Theory X behavior is discussed in more detail in chapter 5, where we will examine positive and strong interpersonal skills. Arguably, a tendency toward this type of aggressive, authoritarian behavior is a negative approach to attaining success. The majority of the people in the United States today who are treated as immature human beings in their working environments are victims of the leaders who continue to display only or mostly Theory X behavior.

This type of behavior has also been referred to as the Bureaucratic/Pyramidal Value System and all too often results in undesirable and/or unproductive relationships riddled with feelings of distrust and doubt as to the efficiency of the leaders. Certainly the people at the New York State organization mentioned previously would agree with this line of thinking.

THE OTHER SIDE OF THE COIN

Theory Y leaders are identified as individuals who are motivated by staff members, embrace challenge, show their desire to be creative, and are not afraid to accept responsibility. This leadership style is known as the Humanistic/Democratic Value System, wherein the leader who has tendencies for this type of behavior will build trusting and authentic relationships. These relationships will help increase interpersonal competence, intergroup cooperation, and flexibility, and this should result in an increased organizational effectiveness.

The Theory Y leader is the person who constantly remains aware of possible negative vibes rising in their surroundings. By working with staff rather than dominating over them, the Theory Y leader tries to find the most effective way to get the job done.

Returning to the Hollywood example, the head of the family, Vito Corleone, was considered a thoughtful and reflective individual, if one could overlook his penchant for things having to do with horses and fish! With Vito's death, his other son, Michael, began to consolidate his power and lead the family by using the theory that Scarnati calls the Godfather Management Theory. Let's look more deeply into the behavior exhibited by Michael Corleone, the character who did display a tendency toward the Theory Y leadership style.

The behavior exhibited by Michael demonstrates all the examples of good leadership techniques needed to bring about the desired results. This may be a bit harsh to think of in the land of academics, but when a staff member undermines your leadership role and tries to make you an ineffective leader, you must take some course of action. Although it might seem a bit of a stretch to say that what Michael did could be interpreted as positive leadership skills, we provide the following illustration of how they coincide with the five characteristics we present as the formula for a successful leader.

- The Ability to Be Insightful—When Michael learns that a trusted person in the organization was planning to assassinate him, he exercises patience and is keenly observant and, by doing so, puts himself in a position of control. He carefully chooses the issues that he wants to confront rather than let his actions be dictated by others. In one particular scene, Michael tells his family legal adviser that he will wait until after his granddaughter's baptism before making the decisions needed to save his life. Although one assumes that saving one's own life would be a top priority, Michael decides that, based on his experiences, he will act when the time is right.
- Positive, Strong Interpersonal Skills—Although Michael generally works on his own, he does consult the members of the family before taking action, particularly in the case of trying to save his own life. He learns to strategize. Michael trusts only a carefully selected few and develops a long-range strategy with these people to further the goals of his organization.
- Self-Growth—Armed with the news of the assassination plot, Michael pulled together all the information he learned on his rise to the top of the family and set out to make a viable plan to keep himself alive. Michael learned from his personal consigliore, his legal adviser, how to stay on top and out of harm's way. Strategic planning is the goal. Strategic goals focus on winning the war, whereas tactical goals focus on winning the battle. It does little good to win a battle and lose the war. Leaders think strategically, and the Godfather was a leader.
- Flexibility—Michael is patient yet decisive. He is keenly aware of his surroundings and, like a chameleon, is able to adapt to confront those who oppose him yet is always willing to explore his options. Neither Sonny nor his brother Fredo possessed mental discipline, and because of this charac-

ter flaw they perished. Michael remained calm and observant while waiting for the right moment. If the Godfather were a real person, he would tell us that the most important trait that a good leader should possess is intelligence—the ability to be creative and to solve problems, or in other words, the ability to be flexible.

- Keeping in Touch with the Community—Michael, like his father before him, made certain that by granting favors, he knew exactly what the community needed, how to satisfy them, and how to put himself in their good graces. While this may seem a bit extreme, it kept Michael always at the pulse of his surroundings. He knew whom he could call on for his benefit, and he knew whom not to trust. To know one's enemy is as important as it is to know those who are in a position to be of assistance. In order to do so, you must be a good politician—get out and talk to people; include people from all levels of the community. And, to paraphrase the Godfather script; "grant competitors the full menu of amenities provided to friends. Keep friends close, but keep competitors even closer—as a matter of fact, hug your competition" (Scarnati 2002, p. 7).

Using the Godfather's theory on management, one just might conclude that his strategies in dealing with his organization can be classified as Theory Y behavior. Of course, in our schools, we can only hope that there is a great difference in dealing with employees while still exhibiting either Theory Y or Theory X management styles. Nonetheless, the intent is the same—get the job done and do it right.

The concept of the Godfather Management Style sounds interesting: a way to resolve issues that appear to be detrimental to the organization and one that would make anyone a successful leader. However, with limited bloodshed, a truly successful leader would have these traits developed over the years through a variety of means, including gaining experience from their own supervisors. We have all worked for leaders who for one reason or another could not successfully handle the power of their position.

Whether an inherent or a developed trait, poor or inefficient leaders are demeaning, insulting, rude, impolite, and coarse. None of these qualities make it easy to work well with others to get the desired results and to win people's respect and devotion—important factors in a successful working environment.

Back to the academic world of leadership: What is the solution? The successful leader must learn to recognize his or her own style of leadership and produce a mix to lead others to produce the desired goals. In other words, they will know how to balance and combine traits or behavioral characteristics from Theory X, Theory Y qualities, and just a little of the Godfather Theory of Management Style.

It is this combination of skills that closely identifies with our findings on the traits of a successful leader. The level of success can be measured by how well a leader is able to motivate others to put their actions into motions that benefit the whole, not just the individual. One must examine one's goals to ascertain whether traits provide a balance of external and internal commitment. Michael Fullan, in his book *Leading in a Culture of Change* (2001), quotes Argyris (2000), who states, "External commitment is triggered by management policies and practices that enable employees to accomplish their tasks. Internal commitment derives from energies internal to human beings that are activated because getting a job done is intrinsically rewarding" (p. 8).

Further explaining the external and internal commitment, Argyris states, "Generating internal over external commitment and external over blind commitment is the mark of effective leadership" (p. 9). In other words, getting the job done because you want to is often more effective than doing so because you have to, which is more effective than getting it done without care and understanding. Pride in leadership drives people to attain goals because they want to rather than because they have to. The successful leader can instill these desires in coworkers through the proper blend of the five characteristics that we describe here for you.

One other important thing to keep in mind is that the atmosphere created by the leader when handling a situation will have an impact on the results. I am reminded of an event that took place while I was serving as the curriculum supervisor for two departments in my district. One of the teachers acted in a rather agitated state of mind because he felt that the budget cuts for his supplies were unjust. His frustration was heightened by the fact that he had to contend with both his principal and supervisor. By the time he went to his supervisor's office, he was red in the face and did not give the impression that he was ready to sit and calmly discuss a compromise.

Therefore, the supervisor took his Theory X approach and tried to quell it with his best Theory Y qualities. Without compromising any of his ethics and in an attempt to reach this individual, the supervisor set out to lead by example. He spoke with the teacher in a soft, but not condescending, reassuring tone stating that he would do anything he could to help support the teacher's needs. As they spoke, the supervisor noticed that the teacher began to feel more at ease—in both speaking with and listening to—and they were soon engaged in a calm, meaningful, and productive conversation.

They examined documented information that demonstrated how funding recently changed and how they were able to increase spending to meet the teacher's needs of the previous year. However, overall budget cuts that particular year made it impossible to repeat the same action. While the supervisor was defending the budget, he made certain to convey the message that everyone felt the impact of the cuts and appreciated the teacher's dedication to his students to the point that he wanted the best possible for them.

Still, the message was clear that the district was unable—not unwilling—to comply with his request for more money. At the end of it all, he approached his supervisor and stated that the nonconfrontational attitude made him feel that perhaps anger was not going to be the emotion needed to get his point across. Therefore, he felt more at ease speaking his mind and a mutual respect was fortified, even though he was not going to get the increase he had hoped for. He left the office with no ill feelings and a plan to make the best of the situation at hand.

Remember, at one time or another, virtually everyone fits the definition of leader. The great leader will be the one who is able to recognize his or her style of leading and find the right mix that will form the combination for success. As with fingerprints, we all are different and therefore will find that we have our own unique mix of styles.

There is no cookie-cutter combination just as there is no one style that will work with every situation. Find your strengths in each style, learn how to mix styles to fit the issue and community at hand, try to lead by example and you will see that the results meet the goals more times than not. In other words, the decisions made and the outcomes of these decisive actions are what ultimately determine the type, or style, of leader you are. As the educational environment changes, so do the school climates thereby necessitating constant adjustments in leadership styles.

KEY POINTS

- John Ivancevich and William Glueck presented a theory of management leadership styles that they called the Theory X and the Theory Y. These theories describe two opposing approaches to leadership—one being aggressive and the other passive.
- The Theory X individual is the micromanager who uses coercion and can be labeled as the authoritarian leader. The Theory Y individual is motivated by his or her staff, embraces challenge, shows desire to be creative, and is not afraid to accept responsibility. There are some points of merit in each leadership style; however, the successful leader will find a workable blend of both.

Chapter Three

One Final Word Before We Present the Five Skills

The purpose of this book is twofold. First, regardless of which leadership-style category most closely identifies your way of leading, we need to examine how to implement the five character traits that define a successful leader. We will illustrate for you how some people employed these traits in today's changing environment with successful outcomes and offer a few examples of how not employing these skills produced undesirable results.

Next, once you have become familiar with the five characteristics of a successful leader and mull over the examples we provided, you will be able to put in motion your own plan to guide your district, school, or classroom toward success for future endeavors by honing these five skills.

TODAY'S CHANGING ENVIRONMENT

As Americans in general become better educated and the fast pace of our everyday lives dictates the need for change, we are faced with new and often difficult tasks placed on us by local, state, or federal governments, parents, and the business world. While the better part of what we do is business as usual, many factors from our overall environment cause us to constantly adjust the way we take care of "business as usual." These new challenges come to us in many shapes and forms and affect what we teach, how we teach, to whom we teach, and why we teach.

The challenges bring with them changes that may be related to redistricting, budget fluctuation, an increase or a reduction of personnel or programs, or any number of things we see in our overall school climate. Technological and sociological issues, such as the need for an evolution from shop class to technical education and home economics to family life and home careers, also play a big role in changes and challenges. Others are affected by political climate, such as the arguably recent increase in violence, not only in our schools but also in our society. Constant changes in legislation, such as the No Child Left Behind Act (NCLB) (2002), the Americans with Disabilities Act (1990), and countless others, also help change the direction in which we operate.

As developing nations rise to greater levels of expertise in medicine, science, and technology and as our role as global leaders takes on new dimensions, we are constantly striving to remain on top—or as close to it as possible. In order to do so, we must ensure that our young citizens leave our classrooms prepared to accept and successfully tackle such demands on our role as leaders.

Finally, as we meet these demands, we must keep in mind that certain specifics, such as the increase in diverse populations, have helped guide our efforts toward adjusting overall scheduling and subject matter to recognize the needs of and accommodate these students in a variety of ways. As we understand more about individual learning styles and the obstacles some students face, we must ensure that our schools are properly equipped and our teachers are highly qualified.

General immigration is once again increasing. According to the Center for Immigration studies, the number of people who immigrated to the United States between 1980 and 1990 has grown more than 40 percent. Those numbers almost doubled for 2010. Therefore, we must adjust our way of teaching to ensure that children whose first language is not English are afforded the best chance they can have for a quality education. Cultural differences must be embraced and understood and curriculum adequately adjusted so as not to offend or omit any particular group.

The increase of international trade and travel also affords great opportunities for cultural exchange, thereby further increasing the need to heighten cultural awareness among all Americans. This idea is one that should not be limited to students in our classrooms but should extend to and engage the entire community.

READY FOR ACTION

Having reviewed the issues, it stands to reason that the first—and most important—step on the road to becoming a successful leader is to identify the changes being required of us from our state, district, or individual schools. Keeping current by taking graduate-level or post-graduate level courses, attending local government meetings, reading the newspaper, and following the news on television, radio, and/or the Internet are all ways to make certain that you are aware of the changes that might be heading your way.

Professional learning communities within your schools ensure that the entire staff is aware of changes and is working toward the same goals. There are many definitions of a professional learning community, as well as many variations of the title. Basically, the goal is to gather together all those involved in addressing and solving a situation. The Internet will be a great resource for you as we recommend that you seek out the books or articles that best suit your environment.

No specific outline of this collaborative group is more correct than another—the bottom line is to find where you are most comfortable. You may wish to start by reading DuFour and Eaker's (1998) book titled *Professional Learning Communities at Work: Best Practices for Enhancing Student Achievement*. Or, you can visit any number of U.S. Department of Education–related websites, such as www.units.muohio.edu/flc, which offers information on developing faculty and professional learning communities to transform the campus culture for learning.

Once you have identified the changes, it is time to examine the challenges that accompany them. Now comes the fun and, often, the most challenging part. It is time to make a plan of action. This takes some doing. Before getting down to the plan, all the issues must be taken into consideration and the people who will be responsible for executing the plan must be brought on board. Now is the time to get ready to start using the five characteristics of a successful leader. We will address each characteristic on its own in the upcoming chapters.

At this point, we are ready to formulate the plan. It is time to pull together those people who would be most instrumental in putting it together and in its implementation. Again, a great tool to help you in this regard is the professional learning community. People skills—known hereafter as interpersonal skills—are going to be your strongest point in getting this task done. After the plan is outlined, it needs, of course, to be put into action. The best-made plans are not worth the paper they are written on if they are never put to use.

Reasonable time limits should be set to identify the results, and then everyone involved should regroup to assess the plan's outcome. If it is apparent that the desired goal was not achieved, it is time to back up, reassess, replan, and reinstitute the proposal. It is at this point where we have to be resilient—to pick ourselves up by the bootstraps and move ahead. Perhaps a little research is in order. With the aid of such tools as the telephone and the Internet, it is not very difficult to reach out to other schools or districts around the country to see how they are handling situations similar to yours.

No matter how difficult or unique the task at hand, rest assured that someone else out there is facing a very similar situation and is either most likely willing to answer your questions or may have already shared their success story, perhaps on a Web page.

Keeping that idea in mind, we must be prepared to recognize and accept that sometimes even the best-laid plans do not produce the desired effect. Therefore, careful reevaluation and readjustment can be made on the basis of the information gathered during that initial course of action. By utilizing the ideas of a well-formed learning community, you increase the ability to brainstorm well and work toward solutions that work best for all.

Do not be afraid of change, do not back away from taking a small risk, and keep an open mind and ear to ensure that things progress favorably. Taking a step back to reassess and move forward is most productive. However, over-assessing and too many readjustments will just create an unhappy or confused group and result in never finally getting the goal accomplished. We will address this further in chapters 7 ("Flexibility ") and 8 ("Keeping in Touch with the Community").

However, if the desired objective is reached, the time is ripe to set new goals. No matter how proud we are of the fruits of our efforts, we must never lose sight of the idea that nothing is ever perfect. There is always room for improvement. Once you have a good plan, go for the great plan. Effective leadership also means having the ability to make an organization stretch to a higher level. And that takes work. A leader does not meet the standard of good leadership or lead the organization to a higher level simply by event or program change. The changes have to be successful and, in order to be so, have to be accepted by those who will be affected by the outcome.

Each time you set out to develop a new plan or to readjust an old one, do not forget to make sure you have all the facts and issues clearly identified and defined. Additionally, make certain that you employ as many of our five characteristics of a successful leader as needed to get the desired results. Turn the expected into the positive unexpected.

Remember the old saying about getting more flies with sugar? After any particular success, it is not a bad practice to offer some form of reward, no matter how small or grand, to let the people involved know that their efforts were appreciated. We will cover this in detail in chapter 5.

Now comes the part you all have been waiting for: our explanation of the five characteristics needed for success, how others used them, and how you can adopt these concepts for yourself. Remember, you may have heard of some of these practices under a different but similar name. It is all a matter of semantics. Most important is that the concepts are understood and put to good use. You may find that you relate very well to some but need to work on others. You may also find that you will want to share the ideas we present to you, with your colleagues.

At the end of the book, in the form of a self-quiz tool, we include a copy of the survey questions that we used to kick off the entire study. It also offers an explanation of how these questions can be used by you—as is or a version you create to better suit your own goals or needs—to help you implement what we believe to be the key to success in educational (or other) leadership. Using this final chapter of questions, you will learn how to assess the answers to our—or your—survey questions and use that information to guide future decision making.

KEY POINTS

- It is imperative that we keep up with the changes in the world around us in order to be able to implement the five character traits that define a successful leader.
- Once you identify your leadership style, you will be able to put in motion your own plan of action.
- No Child Left Behind has presented educators with guidelines and challenges that must be examined and properly addressed for your learning environment.
- Professional learning communities as presented by Dufour and Eaker can be invaluable tools to help you put your plans in action.

Chapter Four

The Ability to Be Insightful

An effective leader should be someone who can recognize future trends and their possible impact on current strategies. Being insightful does not necessarily mean that you have to possess a crystal ball. No one can see into the future. However, the successful leader is one who understands how to analyze past issues and current trends in order to make good choices for future problem-solving issues. One might call this "vision." The ability to be insightful includes having a specific overview perspective for the district, department, or group.

The population of faculty has historically comprised representatives from two or more generations. One can argue the point that in recent years the gaps between the generations has changed greatly, and in order to be successful, the insightful leader will understand how to work across generational differences. Our schools now employ Baby Boomers, Gen X, and Gen Y (sometimes referred to as the Millennial Generation) individuals. Each of these generations bring with them different views and experiences.

It is not practical to try to become an expert on the habits and motivation of every generation. Nevertheless, in order to create a successful workplace, we must be familiar with the key characteristics of the members of the other generations. While the differences are many, depending on personal perspective, we can safely conclude that Boomers come from a more regimented background, following set rules and norms and operate under the expectation that after beginning a career, it takes time and improvement to move up the ranks. This is also a bit of a mystery since the Boomers were coming of age during the height of the antiestablishment era.

As the tides have turned, Gen Y workers tend to be seen as a group who is opposed to following antiquated rules and appear to be interested only in unrealistic goals with little effort to reach them. It seems that the overall expectation is to reach mid- to upper-management positions before their thirty-fifth birthday—preferably, before age thirty. Throughout history, each generation owned their own identities, with subtle changes. One can argue that never before have there been such dramatic differences in the representative groups that form today's work place.

Much has been written on these differences and one must learn to separate the fact from myth. This is especially important since the Baby Boomers are still on the scene, but the Gen Yers, who are all around their late twenties to early thirties, are now becoming the dominate figures in our schools. Therefore, insightful leaders from each represented generation must learn to work together and to use their strongest abilities so as to reach agreements that receive enough support from the whole group to move forward and strive for constant improvement.

However, vision in leadership has to be more than a concept. It must also be an idea that has its roots firmly planted in reality. Budget management, practicability, and setting a reasonable time frame must be taken into consideration before true success can be accomplished. In other words, you must go a step beyond having a vision to the point of being able to make that vision work.

The insightful leader must keep in mind the whole picture —the district, department, or group in which they lead—and work to incorporate as many components as necessary to get the desired results. To gain support from the school board, colleagues, and the community, the successful leader will not only set specific goals but also present a feasible suggestion of how to achieve these goals. This should be done through motivation, encouragement, shared enthusiasm, and visible support for any given project or proposal as well as for all individuals who will assist in attaining the goal.

Knowledge of reform, new curricula, and constant challenges arise from global changes such as cultural and technological trends. The ability to work with these changes will provide for smooth and successful operations. The successful leader must have a clear understanding of both the history and the direction of his or her domain.

Now that we know what we are supposed to do, how do we put these ideas into practice? We will examine a hypothetical situation that is realistic. Let's say that our goal is to raise the reading test scores for third graders. A quick check with the finance people indicates that we lack the necessary funds to increase staffing. So where do we look for a solution? We know that the parents want to see their children succeed.

The secondary schools are concerned that they are receiving children whose reading levels are not up to standard and that valuable instruction is being lost to students who have difficulty keeping up. Local businesses are concerned with the quality of work they can expect from teen and young adult employees. The principal of the elementary school, as well as all of the leaders involved in resolving this issue, knows that during past years when finances were more readily available, the employment of aides for the reading teachers provided the extra attention some students required to help improve their reading proficiency.

Armed with the knowledge of success in the past (an essential part of being insightful) and looking ahead to improved test scores and students who are better prepared for what lies ahead (our crystal ball would come in handy here) yet faced with the realities of the present, the insightful leader will know it is time to turn to some of the other quality traits of a successful leader for the answer. Perhaps the first step will be to look around at what other schools or districts have done in similar situations. In this case, we will imagine that our successful leader learns of a program in place where a core of volunteers are available to fill the gap left by the reduction of reading teachers' aides.

Next, our keen insight allows us to seek out every possible resource in the community that might be instrumental in helping raise reading proficiency. Perhaps the answer can be found by approaching the retired citizens of the community or programs involving high school or local college students looking for opportunities in which they can get involved outside their classrooms. Or you might approach local businesses to form a mentor partnership and use employee volunteers to act as tutors for these young readers.

The truly insightful leader will not necessarily have to personally maintain contacts in all the areas of resources in their community. Successful, insightful leaders will make certain that he or she is aware of the existence of such assistance and that there are staff members who are well plugged in and who can provide access to all those valuable tools that are available in the community.

In the end, the successful leader in this example reaches out to those resources to get the job done. Not only do the students benefit, but costs are also kept to a bare minimum, and the entire community comes together, forming a positive bond that in the long run will benefit all. Any nominal expense would be a small trade-off if the desired result of an increase in reading proficiency is attained. Research indicates that programs such as the volunteer tutor or mentor provide excellent results after being in place for only two or three years.

Being insightful would help in this situation, but a successful leader certainly has to display other qualities that will ensure the desired result. Again, we will get into more detail about the other leadership qualities in upcoming chapters. Generally, our five characteristics need not stand by themselves. Rather, they intertwine and work best with each other.

Back to our insightful leader. While issues that are brought to the forefront by national security or new academic standards are touted as either an original or a supplementary way to address educational questions, the adage that seems to pop up from time to time, that "we have done this before," may surface more often than we would like. The successful and insightful leader must be ready for such reaction to suggestions in change and plan accordingly.

When trying to move the entire district from good to great, we must be flexible with our resources and be insightful enough to realize that we may have to stir things up a bit. With this in mind, let us examine what happened in an actual event that took place in a southern state school district. The highest leaders in this school district displayed their keen ability to be insightful when in 2008 they started a program with the aim of improving the lower performing schools in their charge. What they did was to study the reason there was a disparity between the least and most successful schools in the district.

The conclusion centered on the school-based leaders. So, they began a move to relocate leaders (administrators and teachers) from the more successful schools into the lowest-performing schools. These leaders were encouraged to bring along some of their staff to their new assignment that called for a three-year transfer to elementary and middle schools. To ensure that the higher-performing schools did not face a decline in success after giving up these educators, the principals were limited to bringing three individuals with them for the move.

While we would all like to believe that dedication to education was a sufficient incentive, reality tells us that when people are asked to undertake a task that will be a large inconvenience, something more enticing is needed to bring everyone on board. So, in order to make the move more appealing to these educators, a handsome cash advantage was included in the agreement. All transfers were done on a voluntary basis.

The insightful developers of this program were so successful that when the program was presented, it demonstrated that it actually held such promise that only one leader declined the offer to make the move. Another of the many incentives offered to takers of this challenge was the opportunity to demonstrate the ability to be flexible in administering and carrying through new ideas for and by the faculty at each site. This reward of autonomy is usually well received.

The results of this program are evident in the progress made in the fourteen schools involved in the makeover. Included in the report are that in most of these schools, scores in math and English showed an increase of anywhere from five to twenty-three points, and success was also evident in the sciences. In addition to the increase in academic performance, attendance rose and disciplinary problems fell.

Strategic planning or educational techniques that were once popular may return under a new name or be similar in nature regardless of how their metamorphosis has changed their appearance. Educational leaders may anticipate such issues in light of new legislation, such as the No Child Left Behind Act (NCLB), enabling them to forecast and implement certain changes and techniques in instruction.

According to President Bush, in his 2001 State of the Union Address, school districts and schools that fail to make adequate yearly progress (AYP) toward statewide proficiency goals will, over time, be subject to improvement, corrective action, and restructuring measures aimed at getting them back on course to meet state standards. He called for an increased accountability for states, school districts, and schools and stated that NCLB will provide a greater choice for parents and students, particularly those attending low-performing schools; more flexibility for states and local educational agencies (LEAs) in the use of federal education dollars; and a stronger emphasis on reading, especially for our youngest children. In summary, it is compulsory for school districts to demonstrate accountability of their schools and students.

School districts must ensure that they successfully complete annual testing for all students in grades three to eight and demonstrate the implementation of new objectives that will allow students to reach proficiency within twelve years. Results must be provided in detail and broken out by specific demographics to ensure that no group is left behind. If school districts and individual schools fail to make AYP toward statewide proficiency goals, school districts must demonstrate a plan that will enable them to improve test results and be back on track in giving students the best possible education. Schools that meet or exceed AYP objectives or close achievement gaps will be eligible for State Academic Achievement Awards.

For your convenience, we offer here a condensed version of the requirements of NCLB and how, in addition to keeping current on the local mandates, an insightful leader might start putting together a plan to address each:

1. *Achieving excellence through high standards and accountability*: Remain current concerning all the components of NCLB, and be ready to address each issue. Seek ways to ensure that all requirements are met. Remain in constant contact with the state education department. Form a committee to institute programs that anticipate new trends or mandates, and set strategies to address them.
2. *Improving literacy*: Be aware of new initiatives in reading and writing that will help improve both special education students and general education students. Make use of the special grants and programs that are available to help ensure improvement in those areas. Invite special lecturers to present workshops for teachers on how to incorporate writing and reading skills in all area subjects.
3. *Improving teacher quality*: Explore a variety of ways to inspire all teachers to update their certification or licensing. Perhaps create or

update an already-in-place rewards or celebration program. Set up in-school or district-wide sessions where all teachers not only share information but also lend assistance to those who are trying to update their certification. Equip the entire staff with an easily accessible means to keep them current with requirements they will need to fulfill in order to satisfy NCLB, local mandates, and a current certification.

4. *Improving math and science instruction*: Encourage colleagues to be risk takers and look for new ways to motivate students to take responsibility for, and interest in, improving their content knowledge. Present a variety of possibilities for both teachers and students to participate in programs that promote the use and understanding of tools and techniques related to math and science. Support the creation or expansion of clubs. Get the community involved.
5. *Moving limited-English-proficient students to English fluency*: Be aware of shifts in immigration or migration in your area. If the increase of diverse populations is new to your area, seek assistance from districts that have successful integration programs such as English for Speakers of Other Languages or bilingual education already in place.
6. *Promoting parental options and innovative programs*: Do not be afraid to be a risk taker when proposing new plans. Be visible—let the customer know that you have his or her best interests in mind and that you are well versed on a variety of programs and that you are always open to suggestions. Including student representatives to adult committees in our learning environment can provide a wealth of knowledge regarding trends and actions we can expect to see from our students.
7. *Encouraging safe schools for the twenty-first century*: Know what is happening in the news, keep up with trends in child behavior, and maintain a good working knowledge of the resources available in the community.
8. *Enhancing education through technology*: Encourage innovative ideas in the selection of curriculum and extend the opportunities to after-school hours. Keep abreast of the projected trends for advancement in technology and know what the community will be requiring from your graduates. Find ways to work with local businesses to gain more equipment, get financial assistance, and use their knowledge as a key resource to set up or run programs in your schools.
9. *Providing impact aid*: Since this section of NCLB covers such a wide variety of issues, insightful leaders may have to go beyond their own resources and direct their attention to honing their interpersonal skills to bring others on board and address the issues. That does not mean, however, that insightful leaders put all the responsibility on others, thereby knocking themselves out of the loop.

It is important to always be cognizant of any federal or state laws that pertain to the salaries of teachers and teacher aides; the purchasing of textbooks, computers, and other equipment; after-school and other remedial programs; and advanced placement and special enrichment classes. Additionally, this section of NCLB deals with the funding that is directed to children who reside on Indian lands, military bases, low-rent housing properties, and other federally controlled properties. We will look more deeply into NCLB and its update in chapter 7.

The ability to be insightful is not limited to what goes on in the classroom and to the reform of academic programs but should also be extended to security issues, both national and local. The continued threat of acts of terrorism and student violence have highlighted the need to be insightful with regard to any threat that one can imagine or, as we have unfortunately seen, to the unimaginable. While we do not have that crystal ball to help us anticipate events leading up to the shooting incidents that have plagued our schools over the past several years, there are ways to be prepared.

We must not only concentrate on actions that could be taken by students but also be aware of possible danger coming from outside our schools directed at students, such as attacks, kidnapping, and all forms of child abuse, including that which occurs via cell phones and the Internet. The incidence of such activities sends up red flags and poses a real challenge to keep our schools as secure as possible. If any lessons are to be learned from the recent tragic events, it is that we should be ever vigilant and insightful to emerging security issues. Making good use of the resources that are available through private organizations that specialize in safety and security issues is also a wise step to take. Updating your current safety policy should be done on a regular basis.

An insightful leader is always looking to the best interest of the entire population, with an ever-vigilant eye on the at-risk students. These students tend to need assistance in both keeping up their academic achievement and improving their behavioral development. Therefore we must try to find a program that answers their needs while offering opportunities to the whole student body.

After-school activities are especially effective if the entire community is brought on board. Programs such as these, which provide for either small-group classes or one-on-one tutoring sessions, are extremely effective in providing positive activities to promote productive versus counterproductive behavior. According to the FBI's Uniform Crime Report, there were 9,136 arrests in our schools for simple assault; that number rose to 14,220 in 2004. In 2001 there were 7,860 arrest for drug or narcotic violations and 11,816 in 2004. For both years, the largest number of arrests involved children aged 13 to 15.

When attempting to forecast either security measures or changes in academic standards, being insightful means being proactive, not reactionary. Positive working relationships with local law enforcement groups, as well as groups such as Mothers Against Drunk Driving (MADD) and Students Against Drunk Driving (SADD), certainly help us keep abreast of what is going on with America's youth. Prior knowledge and careful attention to details involving students' trends and hallway scuttlebutt can alert school officials to possible future untoward activity.

There is no need to become an MTV junkie or a slave to Twitter and blog networking. However, staying in tune with the musicians, television shows, and movies of the day and, more important, the messages they send through their lyrics, lifestyles, and philosophy will help you relate to and understand what influences affect our children's thoughts and actions.

Knowing the names of which movies and television programs they favor is not enough. Watch a few of them to become familiar with what is trending. Get an idea of the message they convey. Comic books have played a role in the lives of Americans for more than one hundred years. Today's comic books differ greatly from those of the mid-twentieth century. It is important to know the messages being sent to today's youth and how those messages might impact their thoughts and actions.

For example, the high jinks of Archie and Veronica at Riverdale High have been replaced with Light Yagami of "Death Note" fame. Yagami is a high school student with a supernatural notebook that allows the user to kill anyone whose name and face they can identify. Sixty years ago Superman was fighting minor crime and helping citizens in need. Today he confronts foes such as "Sleez" who turns superheroes into porn stars. Batman's world now includes "Tarantula," a force of evil who murders his nemesis and then rapes "Nightwing." Spiderman now faces the Green Goblin who impregnates Spiderman's old girlfriend while she is still dating Spiderman.

The messages being sent to our young people through pop culture have changed over the decades. Where pop culture previously demonstrated society's new ideas and social values, one might argue that it has now morphed to a point where our thoughts and deeds are dictated by it. Rather than exercise imagination to create pop culture, young people are getting ideas from movies, television, games, the Internet, music, magazines, advertisement, and role models.

Many experts claim that the increase in violence, much of which is now considered the norm, exhibits sexuality to a level where soft porn is acceptable, and gross-out factors and public humility are a joke. Seriously taken or not, all of these negative actions are the central themes of music, movies, television, reading material, and the popular reality shows.

According to the FBI, there has been a 40 percent increase of gang membership in the United States since 2009. Per the National Gang Intelligence

Center (NGIC), juvenile gang members have been known to host parties or other social events to recruit new members as well as a venue for illegal activity. The increase in gang member numbers is because types of gangs have increased. The FBI reports trouble stemming from Hispanic, Asian, East African, and Caribbean gangs that has now spanned out to include nontraditional or hybrid gangs. These gangs, present in at least twenty-five states, have multiple ethnic structures.

Overall arrests for juveniles under eighteen years of age decreased by 23.5 percent from 2001 to 2010 with the only increase (of 5.6 percent) being in the number of robberies. However, in 2010, arrests of children up to the age of eighteen show an alarming number of vandalism (8,617), weapons possession (3,838), and drugs (20,527.) Much like MADD and SADD, there are many programs that have been set up with the intention of demonstrating to our children reasons why they should not fall prey to suggestions that acts of violence are okay.

Likewise, there are countless rehabilitation programs around the nation aimed at helping those young people who did not make the right choices. The responsibility of the successful leader is to keep current with fads and trends. Furthermore, one should stay in touch with the community to ensure that there are ample programs in his or her charge that both deflect these actions and address the situations where young people follow the wrong path.

By no means do we intend to paint a dismal picture of the state of our minors. However, it is imperative that all leaders remain current so that they can handle situations and prevent unwanted situations from happening. Unfortunately, as witnessed far too many times, such as in the most recent tragedies in places like Newtown, Connecticut, or Pittsburgh, Pennsylvania, even the best prepared, most successful leaders cannot anticipate the myriad possibilities of unpleasant and horrific situations that can, at any time, rear its head in our communities. The rapid growth of technology, the ease of extended communication, and the products of pop culture have made our lives more interesting, less stressful and yet much more difficult to combat evil. Cyberbullying, school shootings, sexual assault, and theft all pose constant threats that are difficult but not impossible to combat.

No matter what unforeseen challenge you may meet, our advice is to know what your community is like: what it needs, what it wants, where to turn for assistance and, most of all, avoid knee-jerk reaction. It may seem frustrating, but the best way to reach a successful goal is through careful thought and planning.

The bottom line is that we should plan ways to reach students by borrowing from these venues, accentuating the good and downplaying any negative messages. Although we do not have a crystal ball, we do have many resources that can serve as real tools to help us understand the past and present and make sound predictions. Set the groundwork to prepare for what might lie ahead in our classrooms, in the hallways, or on the playground. Get involved with the community (off school grounds these children are still part of our school), and do not be afraid to be a risk taker when looking to implement new programs or polish the old.

KEY POINTS

- Vision and trends in leadership have to be more than a concept.
- The whole picture, all staff and departments, must be kept in mind when developing your plans or courses of action.
- Look for and use resources to their fullest.
- Issues and challenges may arise due to new legislation such as the updates to the No Child Left Behind Act. Be on top of those changes.
- Security of our students and facilities is an increasingly present challenge. Keep current with the social/political/economic trends that may influence overall security issues.

Chapter Five

Positive, Strong Interpersonal Skills

Successful leaders must model their best behavior when working with those individuals who are in their charge. In other words, they must set an example for others to follow. One should take the time to talk and listen to others. Why? Because we all feel much better when we get the sense that the person with whom we engaged in conversation actually listened to what we had to say. Sometimes the old adage that states that it can be beneficial to be a bit of the guide on the side rather than always being the sage on the stage holds a lot of merit. A good rapport is essential so that individuals might actually enjoy working together. A happy place is a productive place.

Remember in the first chapter when we talked about Theory personalities? The leader with strong, positive interpersonal skills is displaying more of the Theory Y personality with just a tad of Theory X lingering in the background. A little X is good, but knowing how to balance the two is best. None of us wants to be labeled as the authoritarian who uses coercion and micromanagement to get the job done.

Although we are generally presenting you with examples of how developing and using our characteristics of a successful leader provides good results, let us now take a short detour and examine a real-life example of a bad result. In this situation, a person who generally leaned toward the Theory Y side of the equation, out of the blue and without malice or forethought erupted into the worst display possible of the authoritarian, Theory X person. Worse yet, this person completely forgot to exercise those positive interpersonal skills. Here is how ignoring that essential tool resulted in a nightmare.

Our story takes place in a rural area in the mid-Atlantic region. Family histories date back to our founding fathers. The area is replete with horse ranches and dairy farms. Education is a priority, and a strong emphasis at the secondary school level is placed on agricultural and veterinary studies. The total population of the school district, according to the 2000 census, was 55,139 as opposed to 48,741 in 1990. The district was planning to add another high school, but until it was completed, something had to be done to accommodate the new students.

A plan was made, and the principal of one of the existing high schools was delivered several temporary buildings to help with the overload. Without realizing the negative impact of making a unilateral decision in such a closely knit staff environment, the principal decided to move classes out of the school building and into the trailers. Notification of this move was done at the end of the school year—a time when teachers are scurrying to administer and grade final exams, complete report cards, deal with the many other end-of-year tasks, prepare for the coming year, and close up for summer.

The teachers who were selected to make the move to the outdoor facilities were shocked to receive the news with no warning. The overall school climate until then was that of camaraderie so strong that there was a feeling of one big happy family. In the past, changes and challenges were discussed with all staff. Staff members felt that the overall climate had taken a major blow. They were certain that had the principal shared the decision with them, even if the same results were reached, they would have at least felt part of the process. Ownership is important. When a person is made to feel that one has a vested interest in something, one is more apt to embrace and accept it.

Another important issue to examine when talking about positive interpersonal skills is that of sharing. Delegation of responsibilities brings new ideas to the table, gains the trust of coworkers, and reduces stress from the leader. For the good of the individual as well as the system as a whole, an effective leader should also encourage and support continued personal and professional development for staff members. Your coworkers and subordinates have diverse qualities, motivations, and personalities. An effective leader will be one who is understanding and accepting of those differences.

This use of positive, strong interpersonal skills will allow an effective leader to gain the trust of his or her staff by interacting in an optimistic way, even when at times it appears that it is impossible to do so. The effect will be transferred to your staff member when attempting to work out his or her concerns with the performance of their subordinates. Listening, analyzing, and persuading them to reach a compatible decision may accomplish this. Empowering and allowing your staff to make decisions will not only help get the job done correctly but also instill a sense of worth and accomplishment among your staff members.

However, if the decision your staff makes is not in alignment with yours, you should find a way to work through the situation. Incorporate as much of their input as possible so that the decision is not totally one-sided. In the process, do not alienate your staff. Remember that it is important that staff members, no matter at what level, be made to feel as though they are an active and contributing part of your school or district.

Let us now refer back to the situation in chapter 4 where our goal was to raise reading proficiency scores for our third graders. Our insightful leader was well acquainted with the success of the previous program and painfully aware of the fact that it relied heavily on funding that was no longer available. The resources obtainable from the community have been identified. It is now time to set forth a plan. In this case, our leader decides to call a meeting involving the third-grade reading teachers, a representative from the Parent-Teacher-Student Association, a member of the school board, representatives from some of the larger local businesses, the head of guidance or student services from the middle or junior high school that will inherit the students in question, and the head of guidance or the president of the student council at the high school.

At first glance, that might seem like an inordinate number of people, but in our hypothetical setting here, we will say it comes to about a dozen. Each real-life situation will require a different number of people, depending on the situation and the size of the school and/or district. The important thing here is to remember that one of the key things to using positive, strong interpersonal skills is to bring on board everyone who will be directly affected—either by the results or by the resolution—for the situation at hand.

As in the previously cited case of the surprise and unpopular unilateral decision, if you do not make these individuals feel a part of the solution, they may find it very difficult to take pride in ownership. And as we stated before, this can result in only an adverse effect on their willingness to be of assistance. Once our insightful leader informs all present on the issue at hand, it is time to step back and let the group do their job. Delegation of responsibility to others will not only save our leader time and stress but may also provide suggestions from other sources that our leader either was not aware of or did not think of.

In the case of the need to raise reading proficiency, once the leader pulls together the committee, he or she now becomes the facilitator. However, that does not mean that the leader fades from the picture. A presence is needed to answer questions, clarify goals, and see that things are progressing in the right direction. Should it appear that things are not going as well as expected, the successful leader will briefly step up to redirect efforts, all the while realizing that positive, strong interpersonal interaction will be much more beneficial than negative, strong interpersonal interaction.

An occasional verbal approval of the accomplishments of the group will go a long way. Flex those positive, strong interpersonal skills, and show your staff that they are remembered and appreciated. Find funds to spring for a luncheon or staff outing. Recognize achievement by giving out paper awards or public accolades, such as in your school newsletters.

While there are bound to be times when our leader would love to shout, throw something, or dismiss the group to settle things without his or her help, this is not the way to win friends, influence people, or get the job done right in the long run. If our leader in the reading case were to find it impossible to take things calmly or to ease up a bit on the reins and let others take responsibility, perhaps it might do well to take a step back. Now is a good time to breathe deeply, count to one hundred (or more), or totally detach from the meeting. It may be in the best interest to turn things over to someone who is close to our leader and can take over for a while.

We are not suggesting that our successful leader is one who cowers at challenge or is more likely to be found out on the golf course rather than in the school meeting. We do, however, wish to state that we need to take a bit of a stand while learning to blend our Theory X personality traits with our Theory Y traits. We must exercise a bit of both—put our positive, strong interpersonal skills to their best use.

Our hypothetical situation leader may encounter a rough road ahead trying to keep everyone focused and reaching consensus to get the job done. In the end, however, there is the likelihood that the entire committee will be receptive to the plan and that the community, as a whole, will have little trouble adopting it.

The leader in our real-life situation may have gotten the plan done a lot quicker, but at the cost of alienating the staff. Since it was historically such a close-knit group, chances are things will be on the mend, but the healing process may take a long time. In the interim, programs and instruction may suffer. Let us not forget that students are astute beings and that picking up the negative vibes in the school is likely to cause further problems. So begins the trickle-down effect that may prove detrimental beyond anticipation.

The bottom line is to always aim for the positive. Even if it takes a little more effort, the end result will be worth the wait. And don't forget to practice and develop those strong, positive interpersonal skills along the way.

KEY POINTS

- Gaining trust through the use of positive strong interpersonal skills and empowering your employees or staff will result in a more productive environment.
- Verbal and positive rewards will go a long way in creating a tone that will enhance the atmosphere of the work place for both staff and students.
- Remember the character traits of the Theory X and Theory Y leaders and develop a balance that fits you and your environment.
- Aim for the positive even if it takes a bit more effort on your part.

Chapter Six

Self-Growth

First, kudos to you for taking the first step in promoting your own self-growth. Although we should all be in agreement that reading this book will prove to be a most valuable tool, there are many other things we can also do to make certain we are kept abreast of new trends and regulations. This holds true for self-growth as well as any other issues in our lives that we may encounter. There is a lot to gain from reading; however, there are too many resources out there to limit us to the written word, no matter how enlightening it may prove. We have workshops, seminars, audiocassettes, Internet sites, video instruction, brainstorming sessions, and so on that are easy to access, informative, and often pleasurable. The list of resources is almost endless.

Do you try to stay abreast of new trends and requirements by reading something new every day? Certainly. You also should put forth your best effort to attend as many local and nationwide seminars, conferences, and workshops as are possible without totally abandoning your office or classroom. The last time you looked, there were so many e-mails in your inbox from helpful, informative organizations you've established contact with that your district's server has offered you your own domain site.

But the most important issue, the big question, now is: how much of this information and wisdom have you shared with your staff and colleagues? In order to be successful, the practice of self-growth does not stop with you. It must be expanded to include the positive advancement of your colleagues. Think about it. If you have learned something new, if you believe you have stumbled across something that will assist you in becoming a better leader, would it not stand to reason that the most effective action you can take is to share this with others?

Useful information should not be kept secret. Many of your coworkers might have wanted to attend the same seminars, workshops, or conferences that you did but for one reason or another were not able. They may really want to know what you have learned, even if they are reluctant to come right out and ask you.

Of course, it would not be feasible to return from every moment of enlightenment and reenact every detail for those who were not in attendance. Nor would it be well received—we are all very busy and have agendas that keep us from taking in every tidbit of information available.

However, the resourceful and, therefore, successful leader will be able to identify the best way to ensure that information is disseminated so that it is reachable by as many of your coworkers as possible. No one has time to read a lengthy trip report; however, you may find that many coworkers would truly appreciate the opportunity to visit a folder on your district's website to catch up on the latest information you have gathered.

The key to attracting a large readership begins with the subject line on your message. Keep it simple, and let readers know exactly what they will be getting so they can determine whether they want to read on. Personal writing styles differ. But just be certain that no matter how you deliver your message, you must do so in a way that helps readers—fill them in on something you learned that they might also want to know. Reading the results of the efforts of others is one way to begin this goal, but it is merely the first step.

Much can be learned from the written word; however, sometimes the outcome is boring at best. Limiting the way we obtain knowledge from books and other forms of professional publications limits our views. There are many studies that suggest that we retain much more of what we learn by experiencing the information than by hearing or reading about it. With that in mind, beyond reading, we need to make that extra effort to attend professional seminars and workshops.

Successful leaders need to examine all components of promoting programs of self-growth, such as their availability to personnel. Using strong, positive interpersonal skills, you can create an atmosphere where staff members are enthusiastic about continuing to better themselves. A well-oiled machine is the best working mechanism only when all the parts are greased. In other words, for a district, school, or department to strive to go from good to great, everyone should remain current with laws, trends, and methods. They should, to borrow from a phrase from the U.S. Army, let them be all that they can be. It is not enough for management to be on top of things if the rest of the staff is still operating in the dark.

Successful leaders will also strive to work with their budgets so that they are designed to ensure that sufficient funds are available to assist staff at all levels in their pursuit of continued education. If the funds are not readily available, use your resources to get them, perhaps from outside sources in the rest of the community.

Business partnerships are one such way to accomplish this. Creative and well-informed leaders should have little difficulty directing and acquiring funds for self-development or staff development. Sometimes efforts to enhance self-growth will be accomplished through the achievements of leaders in the school buildings, but sometimes there is success on a much larger scale. Successful leaders will use their ability to be insightful, together with their positive, strong interpersonal skills, to make sure that all resources are explored—no matter how big or small.

Now let us look at a situation that is going on at one of the largest school districts in the country. From this example, we hope to show our readers that they should be able to formulate a plan to emulate the actions of this large district by finding ways to fit their personal situations.

Our model district, along with its state department of education, strongly supports the notion of self-growth. Their teachers are required to renew their certification every five years. In order to do this, they must accumulate a large, set number of recertification points during each five-year period. Points can be obtained in a variety of ways, such as but not limited to attendance or presentations at approved workshops or seminars, having their work published, completion of special projects, and continuing education through local colleges or universities.

Naturally, the most points gained for any one action is through the successful completion of an approved college course, as this is the avenue from which one might presume the best instruction comes. Additional incentive to encourage teachers to get their points through college credit is found in salary step increases. The salary scale for newly hired teachers, as well as continued increases, is based on the amount of university credits earned. Significant step raises are awarded for fifteen credits and then again at thirty credits beyond a bachelor's degree, another on receipt of a master's degree, again at a master's plus thirty, and finally for obtaining a doctorate.

However, even from a local or community college, in-state tuition and the purchasing of books can set one back approximately $750 or more—per class. Very often this can be a prohibitive amount for a teacher, especially one who is still in the first five years of teaching where they have not had the time and experience needed to move up the pay scale.

Realizing the financial burden the teacher would face should he or she choose to attend a local university, the district agreed to reimburse teachers for the cost of one university class per fiscal year. While many districts are not financially able to engage in this sort of program, another thing that our model did may be quite doable for us all.

In addition to the cost—regardless of the partial offset by the district—attending a university course can be rather difficult to pursue because of scheduling conflicts, the length of time required, and so on, so our model created its own Academy. The Academy offers class schedules that are in concert with the public school calendars and operating hours and without cost to the attendees. While some of these classes do not offer quite as many recertification points as a university course, the user-friendly Academy schedule and the location of courses—held at K–12 school sites throughout the district—make it so that teachers are more willing and able to attend classes to obtain their recertification points.

The regulations set in place by the No Child Left Behind Act has encouraged the leaders in this district to continue the practice of providing students with highly qualified teachers. Another step our model took was to extend teacher contracts for two additional days per year. These two days were to be used at the convenience of the individual teacher to engage in an approved self-growth activity. The only caveat was that the two extra days of activities could not be done during already salaried time. In other words, the activities were to take place after normal work hours, on Saturdays, or during regularly scheduled breaks, such as during the summer. The cost to the district for this program is much less than reimbursing teachers for university classes.

The opportunity to gain recertification points now becomes something the teachers can do without undue personal hardship. The extra two days added to the contract were paid days—basically an increase, albeit small, in salary. Teachers see this as being much more desirable than having to pay for those expenses incurred which are not reimbursed when they opt for the university course of action. In addition to ensuring that all staff members have the opportunity to continue to shape their career paths, this program opens doors to a wealth of enjoyable and informative seminars and classes available for leaders at all levels. Although the program is new, in theory, it appears that the benefits should prove monumental.

While looking at examples of large-scale efforts, the issue of funding comes to light. To that end, the successful leader must continue to develop budgets that will allow for administrators as well as teachers to attend seminars and workshops. Once that option is available, it is up to the individual to make use of those funds. All too often, administrators are processing papers for teachers to attend conferences but do not travel that road themselves. Administrative organizations negotiate for these funds and as a rule acquire enough money that each principal, supervisor, or coordinator could attend a set number of courses per year. They may elect to attend conferences, classes, or other activities, depending on the district.

But how many administrators actually go back to school for new courses offering activities to build or hone skills of good leadership practices or in fact attend that conference that suggests new and insightful information on improving leadership skills? In fact, the numbers are not as high as they should be. Self-growth is a very important aspect of the leadership process.

Do leaders opt not to go to conferences or other programs because they believe their time would be better spent on the job? Do they believe that they already work long hours for which they are not sufficiently compensated? Or are they expecting to walk into a seminar that proves to be more painful than productive? The question now is; what can be done to ensure that the experience is worthwhile?

We recently attended a state leadership conference at which the expectation of excellent attendance was high, based on the fact that the population of school leaders was approximately 6,500. The number of registered attendees was less than 300. The number who actually attended was even less. The venue was pleasant and easy to reach. A quick glance at the agenda proved promising. What went wrong? Could the low attendance have been attributed to the unfounded low expectations of the leaders who believed they would not come away from the conference having gained a worthwhile experience?

As successful leaders, we must not be complacent when it comes to our own self-growth. Likewise, we should not expect more from our staff than we do from ourselves. In part, being a successful leader means setting examples and modeling good behavior and interest in our positions. We must demonstrate the desire to learn and study new ideology that will help initiate and launch new programs, skills in leading, concepts of scheduling, and ways of motivating and improving the learning environment of your building or district. In the end, our own efforts to promote self-growth will lead to better ways of dealing with stress-related issues and conflict resolution. There is a wealth of knowledge that can be attained through attending seminars and workshops, reading literature, and personally interacting with your colleagues.

One successful self-growth program that we recommend is a mentor and training program for all leaders. When looking into the private sector, noneducation-related organizations make constant training a basic part of the employee process. While many engineers, managers, and employees have on-the-job experience, they know little about the dynamics of the organization. Certainly, the same holds true for newly hired teachers. However, as we continue with our careers, the need to remain current does not go away. Any staff new to a building or district would greatly benefit from a mentor program, no matter how many years of experience that person has.

Putting the two groups together—new and experienced individuals—those new to the profession, building, or district can benefit greatly from the wisdom and guidance of the more experienced. The more experienced, while working with the newly hired, will inevitably pick up information from the recently completed course work, at the same time sharing the ideas brought from their previous positions. This creates a great two-way street. For many training programs, it is common knowledge that the newly hired leaders are motivated to learn about new issues, and this type of learning must be reinforced. No one knows everything, and programs of self-growth promote idea exchange.

Looking at the new employee (a transferee or someone new to the profession), the first months on the job are the most crucial. They have to learn not only their craft but also the ins and outs of the job environment, things you cannot learn in a textbook. Each building has its own environment that includes staff members who are self-motivated or others who become comfortable in their rut and are not eager to take creative risks. They are generally the ones who believe that they have been doing their job well for so many years that the on-the-job experience is the most important and only worthwhile way to do the craft correctly. These people are also likely to be the ones who adhere to the philosophy that new programs are just another way to upset the apple cart.

Obviously, all these negative vibes are harmful and downright depressing to the enthusiastic new recruit. It causes an adverse effect on their colleagues, causing them to become complacent or to jump on the bandwagon to rally against changes. There are those who accept new ideas and new instructional techniques easily. And there is also what we call the deadly faculty room enemy fighter pilot—the one who shoots down the ideas of the eager new teacher or administrator who wants to try some modern way of improving a third grader's reading skills.

Here the insightful leader with strong, positive interpersonal skills steps up to bat and promotes the importance of continued self-growth. A good mentor program will get the job done. Remember, the ideal mentor program is not limited to new teachers but should include new staff at all levels. No matter what your position or how long you have been working in the field, it is essential to learn all you can about the new environment in which you will be working. This should not be limited to your immediate building. Equally important is that you gain an understanding of how things work throughout the district. Your own ability to be insightful will help you weed through all the information you gather and select that which you believe to be the most beneficial to retain or use as a guide in your role as a leader.

The bottom line is this:

- Always work on refining your many skills and talents.
- Look for avenues to promote self-growth and take advantage of the opportunities.
- Share your findings with others.
- Encourage others to engage in activities that will promote their self-growth.
- Create opportunities where existing programs for self-growth do not exist.
- Be a risk taker by suggesting necessary changes to self-growth programs already in place that could use a little fine-tuning.

- Remain current with your school/district environment, including the outside components of the entire community, to assist in the gaining and management of funds to create, change, or enhance self-growth programs.
- Be willing to embrace change, accept criticism, and use your positive interpersonal skills to give constructive criticism to others—in other words, be flexible.

KEY POINTS

- Stay abreast of new trends and requirements by reading something new every day.
- Share the new information you learn with your staff.
- Ensure budgets are sufficient to aid staff with their continuing education.
- Successful leaders must not become complacent about their own self-growth.

Chapter Seven

Flexibility

In our ever-changing society, the latest focus is on customer satisfaction. While this terminology was slow in its acceptance into the world of academia, it appears it is here to stay—at least for the foreseeable future. A successful leader must be able meet the current demand and offer results that will fit the needs of the general public. In this case, the public can be defined as parents, other residents in the community, local businesses, universities, and the like. New state mandates and government, community, and parental pressures require constant change in direction and action/reaction to today's changing climate.

A successful leader must be resilient to meet those demands. In the past, schools have been fairly autonomous in the sense that although there was interaction between the schools and the community, the intensity and direction of that interaction have changed. Recent events have dictated that schools and school districts work more closely with local police, fire departments, and other organizations whose main function is the security of our communities.

Parental involvement has grown to the point where much of our time is spent addressing the needs of the customer. In a survey of nearly 5,000 U.S. principals conducted by the Milken Family Foundation and the National Association of Secondary School Principals (2001), respondents reported that they spent more time each week (7.64 hours) dealing with parent issues than on any other single activity. To be a successful leader and effect change for the good of the community and our students, the ability to be flexible and resilient has increased in importance.

One element of being a successful leader is that it is your responsibility not only to be flexible but also to motivate others to follow the same path. Sometimes you must demonstrate that the benefits to be gained by being open-minded outweigh the minor inconvenience it takes to embrace other ideas. Many issues, such as conflicts in acceptance of revised scheduling, will create resistance and ineffective actions, resulting in unfavorable conditions for our students. For times like these, we need to seek effective ways to operate. Perhaps we might choose to offer a compromise.

We will focus on the scheduling issue since it is both vitally important and something that every leader will encounter at least a few times during their career in education. Incorporating your best interpersonal skills and shared decision-making talents are important and necessary to encourage your staff members to see the benefits to them, their colleagues, and their students.

Everyone affected by a change in the master schedule must be made to understand that being flexible in the acceptance of changes in class offerings, for example, is a decision that is designed to meet the best interests of all involved—the administration, teachers, students, parents, and outside community. To facilitate acceptance, the successful leader will demonstrate how the thinking process should be: If you teach this challenging class or take this inconvenient planning period now, you will be able to select a more favorable class or planning period in the future. Compromise. You, as a leader, must model the ability to be flexible to your staff.

Demonstrate your willingness to change certain philosophies on curriculum matters that the staff might want to use or allow them to carry out trial lesson plans that are outside the curriculum map or sphere of planned activities. Through the proper steps of a program such as the Professional Learning Community, you can show them that your ability to be flexible comes with a positive feeling of allowing them to be risk takers and that you have confidence in their ability to teach.

Our lives are filled with unpredictable occurrences—some good, some bad—but we must learn to meet these unscheduled actions with a plan to deal with them by being able to change our stance. We must be willing to face unforeseen dangers, new requirements we may deem unrealistic, or any number of other unexpected challenges so that we take that situation and work with it rather than against it. Being flexible could include checking what other districts have done with their scheduling issues and working with them to adopt a plan that works for you. We will talk about master schedules a bit later and demonstrate plans that have been successful and how they got to be that way.

These elements of our everyday lives, whether they are in education or elsewhere, further lend to the argument that it is essential to be flexible in our positions, lest we live with having to accept stress and raised blood pressure or lowering expectations. We must be flexible in our way of thinking, or those surprise last-minute calendar, budget, or curriculum changes will put us over the edge, thereby creating an ineffective, indecisive leader.

To further illustrate the importance of remaining flexible, we will present here a few specific examples of how being flexible has played a major role in our lives over the past couple of years. First we will address some very sensitive and frightening experiences that made us change our standard operating procedure in a way we have never had to before. The first is the incident at Columbine, Colorado; next is the terrorist attacks on U.S. soil; and the third is the sniper incident in and around the nation's capital.

As we are all aware, after the shootings in Columbine, schools around the nation began to examine and revamp their security plans. Some schools added metal detectors and security cameras, some began assigning local police presence in the schools, and others put into action a variety of activities to promote positive behavior for the students. Without staff willingness to remain flexible in their thinking, it would be difficult if not impossible to put these plans into motion and, more important, to make them successful.

After the attacks of September 11, 2001, schools joined their communities to increase the intensity of the actions begun as a result of incidents such as Columbine. As if these incidents alone were not enough to make us sit up and take notice, the school districts in Washington, D.C., and many of the surrounding areas of Maryland and Virginia were jolted awake by yet another extreme incident during the fall of 2002—the sniper attacks by John Allen Muhammad and Lee Boyd Malvo.

In addition to security measures already in place because of the other incidents (Columbine and 9/11), a new level of flexibility entered the picture. Parents and school personnel alike now saw the need to keep students protected inside the confines of the main school buildings. Since all the affected districts are grossly overcrowded, most schools include outside, temporary buildings (trailers).

Here the need to become and accept the responsibilities that accompany the ability to be flexible played a major role in that all outside activities, such as sporting events, homecoming parades, physical education classes, and all classes normally held in the trailers, had to be either canceled or moved into the main building. Returning to business as usual had to wait until local authorities gave the all clear that the snipers were in custody and our school grounds were once again safe places for our children.

Without the good examples of the administrators' ability to act quickly—using insight to assess the situation and look for a plan, using positive interpersonal skills to bring their staff on board, and their willingness to accept change—the entire community gained a feeling of respect and were ready to cooperate. With the actions taken by the schools and the close interaction with the local authorities, the incident passed without harm to our students.

Unfortunately, since these incidents occurred, there have been many more acts of violence in our schools. Each time, we learned that the schools in question had taken the proper steps to try to ensure that their students would be safe.

Perhaps the most challenging task educators must face is meeting the requirements of the newest addition to NLCB as seen in the Obama-Duncan Plan. Under the Obama-Duncan Plan we find definitions of favorable actions to include "an SEA (state educational agencies) and LEA (local educational agencies) must commit to develop, adopt, pilot and implement, with the involvement of teachers and principals, teacher and principal evaluation and support systems that:

1. Will be used for continued improvement of instruction.
2. Meaningfully differentiate performance using at least three performance levels.
3. Use multiple valid measures in determining performance levels, including, as a significant factor, data on student growth for all students (including English learners and students with disabilities) and other measures of professional practice (which may be gathered through multiple formats and sources such as observations based on rigorous teacher performance standards, teacher performance and student and parent surveys.)
4. Evaluate teachers and principals on a regular basis.
5. Provide clear, timely and useful feedback, including feedback that identifies needs and guides professional development.
6. Will be used to inform personnel decisions."

One need only surf the Internet to read the many blogs written by educators around the country or to review the articles that have been appearing in the media, to notice that this plan is not being well-received by our colleagues. The arguments against this plan span from questioning its legality to pointing out reasons why this is leading education down the wrong path.

It is important to note that these changes free up the strict requirements to some states. By waiving the acceptance of these changes, the students and administration would have more local power to incorporate real reform and real opportunities to increase test scores. Monty Neill, executive director of the nonprofit National Center for Fair and Open Testing, known as FairTest, disagrees with the Obama-Duncan Plan. Mr. Neill believes that the plan would be counterproductive and has the potential for mishandling of test scores, especially as it relates to student score evaluation and teachers.

On the other hand, the NEA is taking a different view. They believe that more faith should be placed in the fact that educators are constantly seeking valid measurement of student progress. To this end, teachers should have some latitude to tailor their program of studies to fit their geographic/demographic needs. And finally, that our educators deserve to be respected for their efforts and recognized as holding a major role in forming and executing decisions that affect not only the students but the entire local education process.

Right on the heels of NCLB, we are now facing the nationwide reactions, by students, parents, and educators, to the push for Common Core curriculum. One only needs to read the news to note that many responses are not favorable. We see parental protest resulting in increased home schooling. Some people are opposed to the core curriculum, stating that the content violates their right to religious freedom. One of the top concerns from educators is how their class time suffers as the logistic and administrative duties accompanying the program are very time consuming.

However, not all reactions have been negative. Specifically, we turn our attention to a school district on the west coast as we discuss the actions in their forward-thinking community. Students are using iPads as teachers undergo training to learn how to effectively integrate technology with the Common Core. Despite their efforts, there remain concerns from parents in the district. In response, at least one principal found a solution to calm the waters by initiating several actions to meet the needs of concerned parents and distressed teachers.

By being insightful and keeping in touch with the community, the principal's first step was to identify the concerns and to provide a spot on the school's website where parents could communicate their concerns directly and privately to him. The finding was that many parents did not understand the change nor did they want to accept change. Basically, they were not fully understanding of what was meant by Common Core. So, in preparation for their back-to-school night, the teachers were given an explanation to add to their presentation to the parents that included oral, written, and video material.

Additionally, the district created a haiku website for parents that further explained the Common Core. The result was better informed parents who seemed more likely to accept the changes. However, there appeared a fly in the ointment when the parents realized that their students in middle school would all have schedule changes due to Common Core changing the levels of math taught in each grade.

This news also caused new stress for the teachers since they felt that they were not given sufficient materials to help them reach the goals. Teachers who displayed an excellent ability to remain flexible found ways, for instance through websites such as Teacherspayteachers.com, to help them get what was lacking.

The second step, through positive, strong interpersonal skills and self-growth, the principal set out to eliminate these concerns. He orchestrated a series of meetings designed to address the teachers' and parents' concerns about technology and math. In keeping up with the community, they invited the local high school principal to present at the meetings in order to explain to the parents how their children will progress from middle to high school.

So far, the overall results have proven favorable. An open line of communication is in place, and professional development is directed at meeting and improving technology and the standards change.

Finally, we should mention that that the students were also initially stressed by these changes. However, the important thing to note is that some were rather reluctant to embrace the change. But, by following the lead of the more receptive students, the well-informed parents and the professional actions taken by the educators, they are beginning to come on board.

Flexibility in lessons and school planning are also very important as today's children are learning from their parents the importance of being individuals with high goals. This may result in producing perhaps the most creative generation to date. Therefore, it is important to constantly revisit the way we do things to be certain that we are allowing for this creativity to flourish.

Keeping in touch with the community (discussed in the upcoming chapter) can be a challenge as the Gen Y members become parents. One might argue that they tend to be more narcissistic and much less socially plugged in than previous generations. Yes, you say, they all have hundreds of "friends" on their Facebook accounts, but these are not friends in the conventional definition. The vast majority of these friends never actually meet in person or even hear each other's voices. Personal contact has been replaced with impersonal interactions with people who are almost imaginary and who exist only on the computer. When it comes to actual face-to-face contact, Gen Yers generally do not feel comfortable nor are they properly equipped to deal with other humans.

One good trait associated with this type of personality is the desire of Gen Yers to seek advice from others to help them understand both themselves and their surroundings. And the trend seems to be that this advice comes through more impersonal contact via social media networks. Nevertheless, we also see a resurgence of desire to turn to older relatives, such as parents, grandparents, teachers, and clergy. Outside of the family circle, the growth of school and community mentor programs has shown much success. In certain areas around the country, we see young people with a renewed interest in religious group activity.

On one side of the coin, the youthful, strong sense of individuality might prevent the willingness of a Gen Y'er from accepting some of the advice they receive. However, on the flip side, they are at least willing to listen to what has gone on before them and then decide, for themselves, whether they wish to follow this advice. Today it is no longer common practice to turn to books for words of wisdom. Rather, as soon as today's youth learns of new information, they immediately turn to modern technology—meaning the Internet—to verify what they heard and to gain more data on the subject.

In the past, one was relatively confident that information printed in dictionaries or encyclopedias was researched and correct. Unfortunately, this does not hold so true today. In spite of the many warnings that one should not take it for granted that all information presented on the Internet is accurate, the speed and ease it takes to get an answer overrides the desire to investigate further to verify its validity. Additionally, since the young people of today are not well trained, nor willing, to do extensive research, the problem is bound to grow worse before it improves. Therefore, the need for handed-down information takes on a very important role in the education of our children.

Sometimes, when we are exercising our ability to remain flexible, our frustration with others may hit our funny bone in a not so funny way. Many times after trying to understand the perspectives of others, we develop a sense of feeling defeated because we did not get the results we had hoped for or not in the manner we envisioned. These feelings are not reserved only for leaders in education but also are experiences our neighbors in the business world face. Let us take a departure from education for a moment to explore how similar our lives are and how we can learn from each other.

Mr. X worked at a very large retail corporation whose new approach to employee training soon became popular with competitors. In this program, as customers entered the place of business, employees were instructed to stop asking if they could be of assistance, but rather they were trained to inform the customer that it appeared as if he was in need of help. This was developed as a way to engage the customer in conversation and in fact put the employee in an aggressive role as the one in charge.

Many of the employees did not like this new approach and complained that it was a rather rude way to greet patrons. Naturally, the leaders in this company did not agree and continued along this line of working with the public. Not only did the employees find some techniques that they were instructed to use ineffective, if not at times intrusive, so did the customers. Both groups made their position known, but the comments of the employees fell on deaf ears.

At the request of the employees, the company agreed to have them meet with the leaders to discuss their observations and suggestions on how to proceed. At first neither group could convince the other that its way of thinking was the one to follow. Both sides presented their well-researched opinions and their suggestions. At the point of impasse, a representative of the employees, knowing the importance of being flexible, made a proposal that he thought the leaders would accept without compromising the goals of the employees. He was able to present the solution in such a way that both sides of the table were able to come away with a feeling that they remained equally flexible in their way of thinking.

The suggestion was that a fair survey of customers be executed over a one-month period of time and that the survey would present both sets of customer relationship questioning and let the voice of the customers be heard. After the survey ended, the two groups would reconvene to review the results and adopt or renew the training program. The delay of executing the new training program was seen by the leaders as a setback to progress.

But their willingness to remain flexible and pay attention to the employees' concerns seemed to be the best route to follow. It certainly would not have benefited the company if the sales staff were so put off by the new customer service reform that they would become disinterested and counterproductive employees. The employees showed their willingness to remain flexible by waiting to hear what the consumer had to say, which in the long run would make their jobs more pleasant and productive.

This last part was also an important factor to the employees because they worked on commission, and an unhappy customer might not make a purchase and most likely would not return for future business. In the case presented here, the process took a little time. However, in the end, an agreement was reached that did not hurt the profits of the company, did not drive away patrons, and gave the employees a good feeling that they had a word in the company that would be taken seriously.

Being flexible does not mean that one has to bend over backwards and compromise one's own beliefs, but it does mean that patience and willingness to be open will pay off in the end. In other words, sometimes the end does justify the means. Sometimes we see examples, as illustrated above, pop up in our education systems. For example, when unions get involved, there can be times when it would prove to be productive for both sides—educators and unions—to exercise more willingness to be flexible. As seen in our business example, it may take some time and effort, but if new proposals are brought to the table and honestly considered by both sides, an acceptable agreement will be reached. In the case of educators working with parents and students, it would be beneficial to follow the lead of our business example and offer choices when changes are needed.

KEY POINTS

- Meeting the current demands and delivering the results necessary to fit the needs of the general public means accepting the responsibilities needed to address everyday situations as they arise.
- Work closely with local businesses and organizations to create a cohesive community.

- Be a model—do not expect others to do as you say without you doing it, too.

Chapter Eight

Keeping in Touch with the Community

Successful politicians are in with the heartbeat of their constituents. Successful leaders in education must also be attuned to the needs of the community and maintain an ever-present yet always positive place. This can be accomplished by attending not only Parent-Teacher-Student Association meetings but any variety of other community-sponsored meetings as well. Planning and reviewing funding must include the entire community since there is a direct connection between the schools and their surroundings.

While the connections are many, some of the most important are based around issues such as business and shifts in demographics. An increase in a special section of the population—such as an influx in immigration or the increase of the number of elderly residents—could mean a need for a change in certain school programs.

Although each of the five characteristics of a successful leader is extremely important on its own and all do generally intertwine, many times keeping a positive close and constant relationship with the community can prove the most important. How? The best answer: in every way conceivably possible, and then some.

For example, keeping in touch with the business community could be helpful in attaining support and/or funds through such actions as business partnership programs. Local businesses, no matter how big or small, are a wealth of resources. They might provide a body of professionals who supply your school(s) with a mentorship program. Some things these programs can offer are the following:

- Adults in a one-on-one tutoring situation with our students
- A window into the private sector for students of all ages
- Jobs or internships for the older students

- Information/idea exchange between the adults in the business world and the school
- Funds for such things as adding to your technological holdings
- Supplying the actual technology

The latter is especially true when talking about the larger, specialized corporations, such as local newspapers and television or radio stations. They can assist with education programs such as broadcasting or computer technology either by setting up or aiding instruction of students or by reaching the community by providing newspapers or television or radio programs that originate from individual schools or the central district.

Our technology community story takes place at a high school in New England and is explained in detail by Janet Bossange in the book she coauthored with J. Clarke titled *Dynamics of Change* (Clarke et al. 2000). During the early 1990s, the school teamed up with the local university and other members of the community to form what they called the Professional Development Partnership. Their goal was to connect high school teaching with student performance.

The partnership helped realize students' special skills in technology and media by instructing community members consisting of "peers, teachers, administrators, and university interns, how to employ media technology in their daily lives" (Clarke et al. 2000, p. 82). These students, who at one time were still seeking their strengths in a school environment, found their potential by teaming up with their instructor and teaching others. All this was accomplished while developing and implementing a technology curriculum based on the standards of the district.

Emphasis today seems to center around high-tech. However, you must not lose touch with other less technologically based businesses in your area to explore possible ways to help each other. A good working relationship with local construction companies or food or other personal services also can prove to be most beneficial for both the community and the schools. Many schools successful in this area work with restaurants that provide free or reduced prices for catering school social functions as well as academic programs in which food has a role.

It is in cases such as these that it really helps to use your ability to be insightful. Home economics is not the only class that involves food. For educational value, think about how local ethnic restaurants can provide hands-on experiences for your students of world languages, history, social studies, music, and art, not to mention health and physical education. For example, you might consider taking your English literature students to a restaurant that serves foods from Great Britain or from countries mentioned in other works they are reading in class.

In a rural area nestled in view of the foothills of the Blue Ridge Mountains, an insightful leader who has excellent positive interpersonal skills and is very open minded saw a need to make a major connection between the school and the community. In 1990, there were 893 residents of the entire school district who reported themselves on the official census as being of an ethnicity other than white or African American. For the 2000 census, the number rose to 1,438—a 61 percent increase—although the total population increased only by 6,398, or 13 percent. In an effort to help integrate the students of the newly arrived populace, this leader went out into the community in a big way.

Restaurants were contacted to help promote cultural awareness of the places of origin for the newcomers. Shops were brought on board by agreeing to display handicrafts and artwork produced by the students of a variety of ethnicities. Programs were planned wherein cultural exchange would take place in the form of sporting events and musical and drama performances. The results: the community benefits by learning about the diverse population (necessary to facilitate cooperation), the businesses benefit by an increase in profit through the exposure presented by the school activities, and the students benefit through the knowledge they gain and the experiences they shared by creating and performing.

In today's changing environment, one important factor a successful leader must take into consideration is having the local community become part of the school's extended family. Knowing what is out there is only the first step. As we saw from the preceding examples, equally important is the ability to make use of the available resources. This step entails gaining the cooperation of community leaders and parents and a means of advertising these opportunities. Think of the community as part of the school's extended family; treat them that way, and the results will benefit all.

The extended community is not limited to parents and businesses but includes your local government. In chapter 7, we saw how, in part because of our overall changing climate, our schools are in closer contact with local authorities like police, fire, and rescue. However, in general, town governments are where we turn for funds to help us operate on a daily basis as well as to adopt new programs and special projects.

For our final example, we will examine a success story of a school district composed of about 50,000 people located in a state in the Northeast. The results of the joint effort were an Olympic-sized swimming pool, a new field house, and a continuing working atmosphere for future projects.

Representatives from the school district worked with people from the community to set a plan in motion, to discuss the need for the new facilities, to locate a suitable place, and to identify a means for funding the project. They came to agreement that with the school's access to financial aid from the state and the town's access to local taxpayer dollars, the financial end of the project was possible.

The next step was to ensure that the individuals putting forth the project were devoted to getting the job done. This took the passion and insight of some very good leaders. Strong, positive interpersonal skills possessed by the superintendent were demonstrated in the delegation of responsibility to a committee of district staff members and several community leaders. This enabled the district to be a part of all decisions, obtained for the school district the facilities they sought, and allowed the community leaders to give their constituents something that was important to them.

The resources available to a school district are limited only by the ability of the leaders in the district to obtain them. Through good implementation of the five character traits that make a successful leader, goals will be met and the results will benefit the entire community.

Let's take one final look at community relations and its effect on school climate. Even with the best intentions, teachers and administrators can be their own worst enemies. Every once in a while an unintentional comment or a slip of the tongue leaks information not originally intended to go to the media. The most seemingly harmless comment can produce unwanted results. For example, when approached by the media, one might mention that reading scores at their particular school were above average as compared to the norm for the rest of the state.

Although on the surface this seems innocent, other schools in the area are immediately dubbed as sub-par. This could have a negative impact on enrollment as parents hearing of this comparison begin to opt to send their children to the more successful school. The school board and district offices may sit up and take notice and step in to find out if indeed one or more of their schools are not keeping up with the rest.

So, how does one avoid these slipups? When conducting an interview, the most important thing to do is remain constantly aware of its direction. Look for buzzwords or questions that are leading. Never make a statement that makes your side look good at the possible expense of others. If schools or individuals do not meet up to your standards or expectations, then it is a topic that should be dealt with in house, not aired for uninformed individuals to try to address. If you know beforehand that you are going to be interviewed, have as much scripted as you can and know what you are going to say before you say it.

We are by no means saying that schools should be completely autonomous. We must enlist the aid of not only parents but also community members in helping to improve the quality of the school, but there is a time and way to do so. The best way would be to establish a strong learning community as previously suggested in chapter 2. Local businesses, corporations, or even small-town storeowners are helpful in many areas such as by serving on school boards, strategic planning committees, a diversity council committee (described in the next chapter), and school activities.

The values of the community should reflect the values of the schools but yet be diverse enough to include everyone. For instance, many legal issues arise from school-planned holiday activities, prayer in schools, and participation in athletic programs and immigrations laws. Some of these legal issues do in fact go against community values. So what is the school to do? The only way that these issues can be resolved, or at the very least discussed, is again to get the community involved and, using your school's legal counsel, to help sort out the particulars of each case.

KEY POINTS

- A successful leader must know and understand the needs of the community.
- Local businesses can aid your school or district by serving your students with numerous resources such as jobs and technology.
- Be certain that your connection with the local community is of a positive nature for their optimal support with matters such as school programs and demographic changes that affect your district.
- Include the whole community in planning and funding.

Chapter Nine

Bringing It All Together

Now that we have identified the five characteristics that make a successful leader, we need to know how to put these tools into use. We are now ready to take a look at some of the things we, as leaders, are likely to face as part of our overall school climate.

TECHNOLOGY

We only can hope that all of the new technology, which seems to be appearing faster than we can keep up with, is being created to enhance our lives. A few things that immediately come to mind are GPS systems to help us to do things like get around town or locate a lost child, handheld devices that allow easy access to an almost infinite amount of information via the Internet, cell phones that can hook us up to the proper assistance should we have a medical or other emergency, and, of course, things we find in the classroom such as computer labs and Smart Boards.

However, we cannot overlook the fact that it also can present new challenges. All we have to do is read, watch, or listen to the news on any given day to learn how the use of these tools of modern technology has gone awry. Students use the Internet and social networking to assist in cheating, for access to inappropriate material, for cyberbullying—the list seems to add more undesired activity every day. If we try to limit the use of the latest and greatest gadgets in our schools, we leave ourselves open to being labeled technological dinosaurs by students, parents, and colleagues.

Naturally, parents are responsible for monitoring what their children use and how they use it, but students spend the majority of the day at school, not under parental supervision. Under the responsibility we have as guides and role models to students, school leaders must protect and promote those tools for the integrity of the district or school while providing the best education we can for the students. So, how do we make certain that the products used by our school districts, as well as those preferred by our students, are used for their benefit? In other words, the products are used for the good of education rather than as a hindrance to it? Everything we have presented leading to this chapter should point to the answer.

- The ability to be insightful—Stay attuned to the newest devices as they are introduced to the public: what they are and how they can be used.
- Positive, strong interpersonal skills—Understand the climate of your workplace, and decide how you can best approach the many opinions of your colleagues regarding the need for or the ban of certain devices and how to work together with coworkers so that the students' best interests are addressed.
- Self-growth—Research, classes, and/or sufficient training for your staff so will allow them to become comfortable with new technology that they or their students will be using.
- Flexibility—Certainly we should not be expected to accept with open arms all of the new technology we face today. Rather, we must be cognizant of the utility of certain items and be willing to step outside of our routine for improvement. Sometimes, if it ain't broke, we still might be inclined to fix it.
- Keeping in touch with the community—When our students leave our classrooms, they must be prepared to tackle the real world. The skills needed to do so are not limited to reading, writing and arithmetic. The familiarity with modern technology and tools needed to embrace the upcoming changes are paramount. We must keep in touch with the university and business world communities so that we know how to direct our programs and produce successful students. At the same time, we should keep in tune with the requests of the students and their parents. Not only do we need to train students on how to work with the fast pace of changing technology, but we must also make certain that we are addressing the requests of parents. Finally, whenever possible we should educate parents on what their children are using—both the good points as well as the less desirable.

BUDGET ISSUES

One of the top items on our agenda, especially in recent years, is the task of dealing with the dreaded "B" word, otherwise known as the budget. Budget constraints can result in the elimination of special programs such as remediation, in-school suspension, art, music, sport teams, and extracurricular activities. In addition, school bus transportation coverage might have to be changed, resulting in longer and possibly unsafe routes for students. Flexibility on the part of the leader and his or her staff will produce workable solutions to budget issues, such as the following:

- Sharing staff between schools
- New courses directed to replacing antiquated ones as technology and other forms of progress change

Both the execution of strong, positive interpersonal skills and effective measures that keep one in close touch with the community throughout the budget process would do the following:

- Ensure that the public is well informed before they go to vote on budget cuts
- Locate resources outside the schools to help fund programs, such as through business partnerships

Rather than allowing funding for programs promoting self-growth that hinder progress, the insightful leaders might look for alternatives such as the following:

- Hiring speakers/instructors and sharing the costs by doubling up with a neighboring school or district
- Using resources already in place, such as experienced or specialized personnel, to conduct workshops or seminars
- Turning to technology as a replacement for people, such as using computer programs or video presentations
- Seeking grants, not only federally funded ones but also those offered by large corporations

For example, one school we know of recently obtained a grant from America Online that enabled them to install a distance-learning lab. The school, based in the United States, now has the capability to have students work with students and teachers in several European countries, and many different states, and is looking to expand to Asia and Latin America. Not only will this project be beneficial academically but the cultural rewards are immeasurable.

How does a good leader determine the right timing and best way to handle the task of addressing the staff and the general public about budget matters? Leaders of departments at this juncture cannot be too public minded without proper direction from the superintendent or central administration.

However, school leaders who have been in touch with the community and have good interpersonal skills effectively serve as liaison to test the waters to ascertain which programs the educational community could live without until such time as funds are available to restore them—if they in fact need restoration. Perhaps a dignified burial to make room for more current issues might be more in order. If successfully implemented, this will support your district, thereby ensuring your success in being an effective leader.

ADDRESSING CONFLICTS

A good leader has the ability to resolve conflicts between and among his or her staff, nurture their ideas and creativity with regard to instruction, and help develop an atmosphere of trust and harmony in the schools as well as in the extended community—particularly parents. We must search for better ways to resolve volatile issues. When all else fails, take a deep breath before continuing. Of course, there is no cookie-cutter solution to ensure the resolution of all personality conflicts between you and your staff or, for that matter, between themselves.

The leader who continues to strive for improving self-growth as it relates to addressing conflict resolution will do the following:

- Read some of the more recent materials on resolving conflict
- Attend any of the many workshops that one can take to help a leader develop and hone the skills needed to solve problems
- Seek classes, workshops, or written material that explains ways we can understand how to become involved in solving issues rather than taking the easy way by avoiding the problems

The politicking that goes on in repairing severed relationships or relieving tension between staff members plays an important role in good, efficient schools in which positive student learning takes place. A leader with strong, positive interpersonal skills can help heal damaged feelings and calm waters by doing the following:

- Taking on the role of mediator, guide, or facilitator
- Learning how to address the issues rather than the personalities involved

The insightful leader will be in tune with his or her staff, with an open mind, ever attempting to nip issues in the bud before they bloom:

- Look for warning signs that conflict is brewing between staff members, such as differences in classroom management and teaching styles that are not in concert with each other's way of thinking.
- Keep an eye open and an ear attuned to possible problems of your staff outside the school that might affect both their own and their students'

daily routine—such as excessive need of substitute teachers or health and safety issues—and attending specific workshops or hiring speakers with appropriate expertise to help you address these situations.

The inability to accept and work with change results in rigid leadership. Favorable results are better obtained where the leaders know how to remain flexible. New concepts for staff regarding scheduling, curriculum modifications, and changing environments (new classroom assignments) all must be handled by the flexible leader and communicated to the staff in a positive manner. Successful leaders must also remain flexible in the exchange of ideas between themselves and their staff. Failure to demonstrate one's ability to be flexible inevitably sets the area for conflict.

When keeping in touch with the community, one must listen not just to their words but also to their concerns. You must be a good listener and try not to take the criticism personally. For example, a good leader will be able to assess both teachers' and parents' concerns and make every attempt to show understanding and a willingness to work things out together. Here, the better the interpersonal skills a leader has, the bigger the difference in defusing the situation so that there is a workable solution.

SECURITY

We are all painfully aware of how the matter of security has recently climbed the ladder of priorities. The unfortunate reported rise of incidents of students attacking students in schools, terrorism, and random violence in general has created the need for a new kind of leader. Today's leader must be ready and able to guide his or her school or district through these many unforeseen issues. Good leaders are the stable forces of a school community when attempting to prevent tragedy. An insightful and successful leader must negotiate appropriate actions when securing his or her school.

While trying to provide students and staff with good security measures, at times (and much like the present actions of the airlines in terms of security) certain services or even what may constitute staff rights might be challenged. For example, the use of electronic swipe cards for all teachers and staff that allow one to enter the building or that allow a teacher to move from one part of the building to another may have to be installed. This may prove to be an effective and necessary tool but might cause some to feel that their privacy is being infringed upon. The effective leader will use his or her five characteristics of a successful leader to ensure that staff members are willing to go along with this action.

There is a multitude of ways to address specific security needs, just as there are many different kinds of issues. The successful leader will have to quickly examine the nature of the issue, decide on the desired results, and choose the priority of character traits that will be most beneficial for each problem. You will find sample problems and the way in which leaders in education addressed each in chapter 12.

Steps taken should be proactive, not reactionary, regardless of whether forecasting security measures or changes in direction of academic trends. Although the press often paints a slightly exaggerated picture of the security concerns in today's schools, they are not all fictitious media creations. Some do pose cause for action on the part of administrators to reexamine policy and programs to ensure that they are prepared to meet current challenges. These changes can become rather time consuming; therefore, the successful leader is one who knows how to delegate authority and to form committees or task forces to address and resolve such issues to reliable, dependable people, often at a moment's notice.

Changes do and should occur on a daily basis to meet the needs of our schools, and, as we noted earlier (directly after the Columbine incident and again after September 11, 2001), we have had to revisit the way we view everyday life, not only at home but also in our schools. Although each of you has begun to implement programs that specifically meet your needs, a few of the measures taken around the country that you might find useful include the following:

- New security measures might be implemented, such as locking all doors during the school day except the main entrance to know who is entering the building at all times.
- Budget measures might be adjusted to allow a security system to be put in place at the cost of supplies or equipment. Some systems in use today are metal detectors and closed-circuit cameras in and around the school grounds.
- All adults on the school premises must wear visible permanent identification badges provided by the district or temporary identification issued at the school site.

These are actions that call for good negotiating skills a leader must possess in order to persuade both the staff and the public of these measures. These skills are known here as strong, positive interpersonal skills; keeping in touch with the community; and being flexible and insightful.

NEW LEGISLATION

Programs such as Schools Against Violence in Education in New York State, automated external defibrillators (AEDs), the No Child Left Behind Act

(NCLB), school voucher programs, and national standards constantly give cause to adjust our means of attaining our educational goals. The new legislation mandates can be especially taxing to you as a leader, and again budgets must be realigned to help defray the costs. One such example is in a large school district on the East Coast where the requirement to meet the NCLB mandate caused a $26 million deficit in its budget for the 2003–2004 fiscal year. Most of us agree that this is unacceptable and a great hindrance to achieving the goals of providing the best education to our students.

As in this case, many other districts nationwide have had to find the funds with little or no federal or state relief to help implement these programs. In one school district alone, more than $100,000 was spent to implement the state mandate of having AEDs in their school buildings. They realized that a local sports complex might also have use for the AEDs. When dealing with the AED issue, the insightful leaders, aware that the funding was originally to come from the sports complex, were able to employ their strong, positive interpersonal skills to demonstrate to all involved how this joint venture would be beneficial.

Therefore, by keeping in touch with the needs and activities of the community, all parties agreed that by keeping an AED on the sport complex premises, it would be in place for the students and, at no cost to the public, would be available to them as well should the need arise.

This is a good example of a win-win situation in which the needs of the school district and the general public were met with minimum cost to the school district. A successful leader must use all of his or her leadership skills to balance the sacrificing of one spending project for another. The school district did not have an arena—the community did. The district needed an arena, and the community benefited from the AEDs onsite.

In addressing issues relating to new legislation, the successful leader must be ready to accept change knowing that the change might not be well received and that, in this case, the circumstances are different than other situations in that we have no direct control over what directives we are asked to follow. Some courses of action that would help the acceptance, implementation, and success of these new mandates are the following:

- Self-growth—Make certain that local policy and regulations are clearly stated to facilitate interpretation and to follow the intentions of the governing body that issued the mandate. Ensure that sufficient information is disseminated among staff so that they are kept up to date.
- Flexibility—More important than a willingness to demonstrate your acceptance of new legislation is that you never let your staff think that they are the only ones who will have to be flexible in order to meet new challenges. You too must show your efforts to work to implement these laws or regulations.

- Strong, positive interpersonal skills—While trying to win over your staff, you must remember that the Theory X personality will have a more difficult time convincing people to cooperate, even though the Theory X person might get the job done. The accountability issue for raising test scores as prescribed by NCLB and the new emphasis on Common Core curriculum has the potential to stir up bad feelings and reactions from classroom teachers, not to mention added pressure from parents. By keeping all parties working harmoniously together, more desirable results will surface.
- Keeping in touch with the community—Working through the school board and Parent-Teacher-Student Association (PTSA) meetings, parents must be brought on board regarding any changes that will affect the future of their children.
- Ability to be insightful—Keeping abreast of current trends might serve as a warning signal that new legislation is on the horizon. Keeping in contact with the state department of education, county legislators, local police, and emergency operations officials could provide good insight to what might lie ahead.

DIVERSITY

The diverse population of the district can dictate the action or reaction of teachers or administrators. It is essential that successful leaders handle diversity issues with sensitivity and a demonstration of strong concern as well as an interest in making sure all parties feel that a fair resolution has been achieved or at the very least attempted.

To illustrate the importance of addressing diversity issues, we will visit a situation that had the potential to become a problem in one district and how the leader addressed and resolved the concern. He stated that the ways we react to diversity, whether it has to do with gender, race, religion, ethnicity, or disabilities, share similar traits. In one particular situation of possible racial prejudice, it was the perception of concerned parents that the school in question was not addressing this issue properly. An incident had occurred in which parents believed the school unjustly favored one participant over a minority student.

Using his five characteristics effectively, the leader addressed the issue as follows:

- The ability to be insightful—The leaders in this district were keen to note that the handling of this was an incident of extreme importance. The administrator in charge believed that rather than trying to analyze the situation through the eyes of the minority groups in question, the better

course of action would be to determine how he, based on prior knowledge and experience, could resolve the issue.
- Self-growth—The administrator examined the history of his own abilities and shortcomings in relating to other diverse cultures and tried to determine why he had not attained the desired goal. This, coupled with an effort to study racial diversity models, brought about favorable results.
- Keeping in touch with the community—The willingness of the leader to keep abreast of the needs of and changes in the community helped him reach out to the people as someone they knew and trusted, not as a stranger. The result was that all parties gained a better understanding of what each group had to bring to the conversation, facilitating mutual understanding and reaching a desired goal.
- Strong, positive interpersonal skills—These skills helped him bring a more acceptable working climate to the building. He worked with his staff regarding how they could be more open and how they could listen to others with a different point of view and renounce their real or perceived negative attitudes.

The administrator stated, "You, as a leader, must invite others into your building with an attitude of a welcoming spirit. Based on that, we established a diversity council in our building to look at sensitive issues of racial diversity programs and invited parents and community members in to talk about how the kids and they themselves feel when they walk into a predominately white building."

By admitting that things have to change to obtain positive results and remaining sensitive to the needs of people from a variety of diverse backgrounds, you will gain success in your attempts to rectify the problems you face and to increase the number and the success rate of new and effective programs. If people are made to feel that they are listened to and supported, you will gain their trust and cooperation. The leader in the previously cited example realized that one must examine and properly choose any or all of the five traits to help address each situation as diversity issues arise.

The bottom line: as a successful leader, you must be insightful to help make a connection with your own feelings. Additionally, you must remain flexible to ensure that you are encouraging an acceptance of diverse cultures in your building by your entire staff and students.

STAFF DEVELOPMENT AND MENTORS

Successful leaders must have the ability to encourage and motivate their employees through a series of staff development opportunities and by their own efforts to model this behavior. This will promote an atmosphere where learning is valued.

In a time when budget constraints are all too prevalent, distribution of funds should include sufficient resources to provide for staff development programs in concert with the size and needs of the school or district. There are many ways we can meet the requirements set forth by NCLB, wherein schools are required to provide their students with only those teachers who are considered highly qualified. Each state has been actively working to find ways to ensure that all their teachers fit the requirements necessary to meet the NCLB standards of being highly qualified.

State departments of education now require that all teachers are teaching the exact subject for which they are licensed (certified). Some require their teachers to renew their certification every so often. Principals are being held accountable for the students in their schools by having to prove student proficiency on standardized tests. This may include the entire student population regardless of the numbers of special education students at each school. Failure to meet this requirement will guarantee that the principal is out pounding the pavement.

These issues have caused administrators around the nation to find ways to support their staff, keep them current on educational trends and issues, and ensure that all students are learning to the absolute best of their ability. The successful leader must employ all five of the positive leader traits to set up programs to fulfill these requirements and ensure their own job security.

Although there were many programs introduced to each school, one of the most successful has been the teacher mentor–mentee program. To support mentor-mentee programs, a successful leader must address and resolve such issues as time release, salary implications, and selection of mentors. In doing so, the following will be accomplished:

- Their ability to be insightful will help guide them to meet future needs
- Their positive interpersonal skills will encourage teachers to work together to perform at their best
- Their own self-growth is essential to lead their staff in their pursuit of this goal
- Remaining flexible to accept suggestion and embrace change is paramount to success
- Keeping in touch with the community to ensure that their needs are being met will undoubtedly result in excellent programs and students who are learning at their optimum ability

STRUCTURING

Proper structuring is the key to success of any business, school districts not excluded. The idea of structuring encompasses a wide spectrum of issues, from creating area divisions within a school district (clusters) to the setup of both physical and academic course structuring (Professional Learning Communities [PLCs]) inside a single school building. Each kind of structuring is in place to accomplish a specific goal, such as effective management in large areas (based on the number of students), programs that are understood and uniformly practiced within the district or school, and so on. To better illustrate what we are talking about, we offer the following success stories.

The first concerns four urban school districts. We learned about these districts via the Council of the Great City Schools, a coalition of sixty-four of the nation's largest urban public school systems, whose headquarters are in Washington, D.C. Their efforts have resulted in a rise in overall academic performance. These districts are the Houston Independent School District (Texas), the Charlotte–Mecklenburg School District (North Carolina), the Sacramento School District (California), and the Chancellor's District in New York City. It appears that the secret to their success lies in seven important steps:

- Measurable goals for the district and its individual schools with timetables for performance—ability to be insightful
- Accountability systems starting at the top that hold staff responsible for results—flexibility
- District-wide professional development for teachers and staff on implementing the curriculum—self-growth
- Systems for monitoring the implementation of reforms in the classroom—ability to be insightful
- Regular testing and detailed data to measure progress, assess weaknesses, and intervene before students fall behind—ability to be insightful
- Initiation of reforms in the elementary grades, working up to the middle and high schools—flexibility and keeping in touch with the community
- Focus on the district's lowest-performing schools and groups—all five skills

For more information on its formula for success, you can visit the Council of Great City Schools at www.cgcs.org/reports/foundations.html.

Next, let us explore clustering, an idea that seems to be working well for very large districts. In a cluster system, the district is divided into mini-districts, sometimes called pyramid clusters, each composed of high schools and their feeder elementary and middle schools. A director leads each pyramid cluster. The director of each pyramid cluster does the following:

- Monitors, assesses, and evaluates school effectiveness to ensure that a high-quality instructional program is provided for all students.
- Monitors student achievement and implementation of the program of studies
- Directs the provision of student services
- Evaluates principals
- Responds to parental concerns that cannot be resolved at the local school

In order for a system such as the cluster concept to be successful, it must be staffed with highly qualified leaders who understand how to employ the five leadership characteristics.

Finally, when considering issues of structuring, we can once again turn to concepts that call for the need of a clearly defined school system. Specifically, we are referring back to the PLC. Therefore, a school or district has to be properly structured, and this structuring must include the entire community. DuFour and Eaker (1998) explain that antiquated systems of education—such as the industrial model of the early 1900s—were good for their times, but as the world progresses, so does the need arise for change in the way we operate.

The PLC emphasizes the importance of bringing together all individuals necessary to get the job done. They define the PLC as having six basic components. As we list them here, you will note how they correspond to the five characteristics of a successful leader as we have defined throughout this book. While the PLC requires the involvement of all parties concerned, each one—a leader in his or her own right—has the responsibility to exercise the five characteristics as they fit in:

- A shared mission, vision, and values—ability to be insightful
- A collective inquiry—keeping in touch with the community
- Collaborative teams—positive, strong interpersonal skills
- Action orientation and experimentation—flexibility
- Continuous improvement—self-growth
- Results orientation—flexibility

COMMUNITY RELATIONS

No matter how adept an administrator is in matters such as finance, classroom management, and curriculum structuring of after-school programs, if that person is unable to establish a good relationship with the community, his or her efforts are wasted. By the community, we mean any group that affects the goings-on of the school or district, such as the school board, a concerned taxpayer's group, the PTSA, local businesses, or the staff.

When letting the public know about the successes and challenges of your district, there are several significant issues for a successful leader to take into consideration. Opening a pathway to the public for accessibility to the inner workings of a district meeting can be complex as some topics, such as test scores, redistricting, and personnel, might be highly flammable. How does a successful leader handle complex situations?

In August 2000, a television news program reported a suicide of a newly hired school principal. The public relations department and the superintendent acted in tandem to ensure that the media got what they required while the school district gained respect from the media for not hiding facts. The superintendent worked with the media and agreed that time would be allotted for them to report the story only after all the initial investigation by the district took place and that full access would be granted without interference by the district.

After the district finished its investigation, the superintendent gave the go-ahead for the media to come in and do its reporting:

- The good leadership style of this superintendent not only gained what he wanted but also provided the entire community the information they both needed—keeping in touch with the community.
- His experience of past dealings with the media and a logical plan allowed him to be successful in this very tragic situation—ability to be insightful.
- Leaders sometimes fear the media. It is a natural human reaction to want to keep outsiders away from personal information. However, by being flexible in this matter, this superintendent was able to step aside and let the media do its job—flexibility.
- Successful leaders have good relationships with the media, which then creates an atmosphere of mutual respect and fair, equitable treatment. By meeting them halfway, this leader was able to build and maintain the ever-important respect of the local media—positive, strong interpersonal skills.

All too often, we experience tragic accidents that involve the premature fatality of our students. Given the popularity of student cell phones and therefore the rapid ease with which information can be disseminated, there is a constant race to squash rumors before they become uncontrollable. In one such incident, the information of an automobile accident spread to other students quickly. At the same time, the media got word via their scanners. The school district was actually the third party to know about the accident. It was important, therefore, for the district to take action and contact the media right away. To gain control over the distribution of information, the district contacted the newspapers and radio and television stations and set up a press conference:

- The media were invited into the building with the provision that they respect the rights of the students to mourn their classmates and not interview students in the school building—positive, strong interpersonal skills.
- Recognizing that time was needed to put all the pieces together, the media could not enter the scene until the school officials were ready—ability to be insightful.
- Coupled with the previous two characteristics, this one was especially important because parents needed to be contacted before they received news of the accident via the rumors that were already being passed around—keeping in touch with the community.

In this case, instead of the district's being fearful of the media coming onto the premises and interviewing students without approval, the schools' leaders took control of the situation and focused the media on the district's direction of the situation. Already developed, good leadership skills and well-established, positive relationships will help during those times you do not have ample opportunity to address issues, particularly sensitive ones, with the luxury of sitting back and reflecting on and analyzing how to proceed. Although all of the above outlined is important, we realize that with the popularity of cell phones, security cameras, and YouTube, we may often find ourselves frustrated to learn that all of our good efforts may not result in our intended goals.

Another example involving the importance of a good relationship with the media took place in a district that, although not near Washington, D.C., was affected by the 2002 sniper incident there. Students who had been on a field trip to Washington were scheduled to return to their home district at approximately midnight. The media were extremely interested in interviewing these students on their return.

Because of the district's good relations with the media, they respected the request to allow the students some time to connect with their parents before being interviewed. If contacts at the media know that you are a leader who is honest and interested in their feedback and needs, you will gain their trust and build solid relationships that will prove to only help your district in future circumstances.

Unfortunately, this did not seem to work well at the December 2012 shooting incident in Newtown, Connecticut. Days after the shooting, parents and other concerned citizens begged the media to ease off. However, even though some reporters were quoted as saying they were uncomfortable with their relentless coverage, the withdrawal of media attention was painfully slow.

Good leaders in situations such as these also need to be flexible. Both flexibility and resilience are important because they will lead to what is best for the district's constituents. Additionally, successful leaders will keep in mind the community needs when scheduling appointments or other such events. This will show the community that you respect them and their time, thereby going a long way in building the relationships necessary to solve the issue at hand.

UNIONS

The effective use of the outlined qualities of a successful leader will provide your administrative unit the effective tools needed to maintain a good workable relationship with the different employee unions. This is a topic that many of us hold dear to our hearts. How does the successful leader enter this sensitive area, which includes tenure as well as other personnel issues, with integrity, patience, understanding, and, yes, a good attorney? What, therefore, are the character traits a successful leader needs to effectively carry out initiatives of the administrative leadership and maintain good relations with unions?

In these, as in all situations, a successful leader might use one or the entire list of the five characteristic traits to help resolve tense feelings that sometimes grow at meetings held between administration and employee unions:

- One might use self-growth and the ability to be insightful to reflect on the discussion of those meetings.
- Excellent interpersonal skills will help mediate those intensive discussions and will be beneficial to all involved.
- The ability to be insightful and keeping in touch with the community will help resolve conflict by knowing what the staff desires. When anticipating future grievances use information gained from past union meetings and formulate new logical plans to proceed.
- A successful leader might use flexibility and keeping in touch with the community as well as a certain resiliency to his or her own efforts. He or she then can continue with what he or she perceives to be the right thing to do based on other organizations in the area as well as other school districts.

In our article "Profiles of Leadership" (Jacobs and Langley 2002), we briefly outlined the steps that four administrators used to achieve their goals and how they did so by employing the five characteristics of a successful leader. In the next chapter, we will demonstrate, in detail, how five administrators and one business leader used these skills to achieve success working with unions and master schedules and putting new programs in motion.

KEY POINT

- There are many factors that we face on a regular basis that require our attention and action. You must be certain to try to implement the five essential skills to guide you through budget issues, addressing conflicts, security concerns, new legislation, diversity both in the school and community populations, staff development, mentors, structuring, community relations, and unions.

Chapter Ten

Now What?

Now that we have identified some issues we deal with and the five basic traits we as successful leaders need to possess in order to address them, how do we know that they work? In this chapter, we will examine six examples of successful leaders in education and how incorporating these characteristics, to a great extent, attributed to their success with issues with which they were faced in the course of their careers. Five are administrators in the field of education, and one is from a business that is not related to education.

We have decided to add the last to illustrate that these characteristics work for all leaders, no matter the setting. Finally, our examples cover issues that affected as few as a hundred people to almost ten thousand. Our intention is to provide examples that can be easily adopted and adapted to situations you may encounter.

Our first example is that of a now retired assistant superintendent from a suburban school district with a population of roughly 52,000 residents. The school district itself comprised of student body of approximately 8,700 children. A problem existed for years between the school district and the local union. These two organizations were at odds about a number of personnel issues. Little progress was made when it came to discussions about working conditions, salary increases, and finally how the process of negotiations should take place. Exercising his ability to be insightful and flexible and enhancing his and his colleagues' opportunities for self-growth, he sought assistance from a company called ThoughtBridge.

ThoughtBridge is an organization that specializes in helping clients to manage change, conflict resolution, and negotiation. By utilizing their techniques, this administrator and his colleagues were able to substantially reduce the number of grievances and opened the door for resolving future issues in a fair and democratic manner. In this case, proper utilization of the five characteristic traits of a successful leader, in concert with ThoughtBridge, helped solve or, at the very least, ease the tension and problems of both the district and the union. If you would like more information on ThoughtBridge, we suggest you visit their website at www.thoughtbridge.net.

By using good leadership traits such as good interpersonal skills—the ability to be insightful and flexible—this administrator helped negotiate a labor contract in only five days. Through sound judgment and his ability to be insightful, he decided that new strategies and conditions needed to be put in place so that a culture of trust and improved relations could exist. He put into motion the following strategies, which allowed for improved communication:

- Provided easy access to district leaders, including an open-door policy that allowed positive discussions to take place at any time
- Moved to a new method of problem solving based on interests of parties as opposed to standing positions, resulting in less confrontations on issues
- Empowered schools and individuals to take a leading position in ironing out their own differences
- Engaged joint training in problem-solving tools
- Set each organization up for success by supporting the leaders of the two units

Thanks to his ability to successfully employ positive leadership qualities, the result was an improved atmosphere in which historically opposing units were able to work together.

Another example of how a successful leader employed these skills comes from a moderately sized suburban school district. This time we will look at an accomplishment of a principal of an elementary school. In this case, the issue was that the building staff was upset and concerned that their grade level was not getting a fair shake when it came to putting together the master schedule. Our principal used good problem-solving skills not only to satisfy the staff but also to enhance the master schedule.

For years, putting together the schedule was a unilateral decision, in this case a task that was always performed by our principal. However, with the beginning of each new school year came a variety of complaints regarding how unfair the schedule was to certain grade-level teachers. Exercising strong, positive interpersonal skills, the ability to be insightful, and keeping in touch with the community, our principal's new strategy was to gather the teachers who knew how to work within the confines of the master schedule. A committee was formed of teachers from each of the grade levels, special area teachers (music, art, and physical education), and a teaching assistant.

Serving at first as the facilitator of the scheduling committee, the principal then stepped back and allowed the teachers to work out the scheduling. Providing release time during the day for the teachers, so that they would have the opportunity to work together on the program, gave the teachers the feeling of ownership in the program. Additionally, by providing this extra time, the principal demonstrated that flexibility was needed across the board in order to get the desired master schedule put together and then put into action.

The results, in our subject's own words, were that "we put together a schedule that was a vast improvement over anything I had done previously." The principal further stated that in addressing the situation this way, the teachers gained a positive feeling that they were instrumental in the resolution and had a personal investment in the project. A five-day rotating schedule replaced an antiquated four-day schedule, allowing for more time for musical groups and enrichment opportunities in physical education and art. It also created a library and computer period for students in grades K–3.

The success of this new scheduling initiative was based on the principal being willing and able to delegate, to employ positive interpersonal skills, and to be flexible in accepting new ideas for scheduling. The community in this case was the teachers, the students, and the parents. By remaining aware of what was needed for each component of this community, the master schedule that was created suited them all.

Keeping with the theme of master scheduling, we move our attention to another suburban district that is part of an overall very large metropolitan area. The master schedule in this case was for a middle school. Several of the classes taught at this school are high-school-credited programs. Our administrator for this example held the title of director of student services and was tasked with overseeing the education process of roughly 1,380 seventh and eighth graders in a school building that was constructed to house 1,000. The incredible increase in the number of businesses and residences in the area over the previous eleven years produced an equally rapid flux in the growth of the number students attending this school.

The challenge here was how to develop a workable master schedule that would be most beneficial to the students and incorporate a team of teachers who were highly qualified. The first step began with self-growth. By chance, this administrator had become involved in a program initiated by then president George H. W. Bush that addressed issues surrounding the infrastructure of our nation's schools. Sharing the knowledge gained via this venue with colleagues at the school greatly enhanced their understanding of meeting the needs of the students and protecting the positions of the teachers.

The next step was the identification, adoption, and implementation of a software program designed to record statistics and information on attendance and grade reporting. While using the software, our administrator did not forget about using good leadership skills. Close contact was maintained with the community to monitor the population for changes and growth. A clear demonstration of the ability to be flexible and use foresight was employed to help recognize and address the importance of meeting the needs of the community while incorporating instructional techniques that were user friendly.

The end result was a program of a partial-block schedule that is still in place some ten years after its inception. The schedule allows for changes at a moment's notice without disruption of the educational process. As the need arises for attention to shift to certain activities—including remediation programs during the course of the school day, in and out of school field trips, and so on—teachers, students, and mentors can accommodate these needs with ease. Standardized test scores have risen. The need for student disciplinary actions has waned.

Our next example of a successful leader was a principal of a high school in a citylike setting in a suburban area on the east coast. At one point, the school had an international baccalaureate (IB) program in place, but the program failed. The new principal arrived at the school determined to reinstitute the IB program with strong positive feelings that this time it would be a success. To do so, our principal had to be insightful, possess good interpersonal skills, remain flexible, and keep in touch with the community. The first step was to gain support for the program by reaching out to the community to help put together meetings between parents and faculty and incorporate their thoughts and comments, thereby giving them ownership of the program.

Throughout the process, our principal was not hesitant to delegate responsibility, and we quote: "Successful leaders are confident in their staff and are willing to demonstrate that confidence to them." These efforts were successful. The IB program initially served a small number of students, and through the combined efforts of students, parents, and faculty, they tripled the size of the program, not to mention increased its acceptance and produced excellent test results.

Our final example of a leader in the field of education tells of the birth and growth of a very successful program established by a small group of some very insightful people. Around the last part of the 1990s, this group, while working on the assessment process of all second-language students, wondered how one could be certain that the progress of students learning a second language was fairly assessed and that all students were learning all they could. Working with the American Council on Teaching Foreign Languages guidelines as a place to begin, they formed a plan. As we spoke with one of the people from that group of organizers, she looked over the list we had put together on the five most important leadership skills and began to chuckle.

She told us that it was as if we were flies on the walls of the offices as the language team went to work on the assessment program. She said that she found each and every one of these five skills to have played a major role in the formation and implementation of the program. Her story followed our theme so closely that it is presented to you here in its entirety:

> We took a look at ourselves and asked: how do we know that students are performing equally at each school in our district? In order to answer this question, many things had to be done, starting with looking at our assessment tools and curriculum without appearing as though we were questioning the ability of our teachers.
>
> The ability of the staff to be insightful greatly aided as we put forward to formulate a program that would provide the best possible opportunity for students to come away from our language program with as much proficiency as possible in the areas of speaking and listening as well as in their ability to read and write the target language. We determined that our goal was to produce communication proficiency at its best.
>
> If you think positive, strong interpersonal skills had a large role in this endeavor, you are very correct. Not only did the staff have to put together the program in such a manner that it would prove effective, but we had to work well with our teachers, the administrators, local universities, parents, and students to ensure that we were able to demonstrate to them how valuable a tool our new program would certainly evolve into, in a relatively short time. We had to work with administrators to reinforce the idea that there would not be an undue hardship placed on their already suffering budgets.
>
> We had to work with the parents to ensure them that this new program would benefit their children as they prepare to enter quality universities or to enter the workforce. We had to work with teachers to be certain that they did not feel as though we were asking them to make changes that would take away time from their already busy day or to convince them that the new program would not be creating micromanagers from the people on my staff.
>
> Our entire staff had to remain very flexible, as we repeatedly had to step back and evaluate our process. Then, as the program went into place, verify that we were all on the same page, heading toward the same goal.
>
> As for self-growth, well, we had to be certain that we were all in tune with current trends and expectations at the college level so that we could create not only a program that worked but also a rubric that made sense and accurately measured students' progress. I suppose we did okay since we now see that many schools and universities around the country have adopted the rubric and appear to be very pleased with its results.
>
> Finally, keeping in touch with the community was and remains also key, as we must ensure that the proficiency of students continues to meet or exceed our original expectations and that the customers—the parents, students, and community at large—remain pleased with the fruits of our efforts.

The program in our example is called Performance Assessment for Language Students (PALS.) If you are interested in learning more about this second-language acquisition program, you can visit www.fcps.edu.

Before we leave this chapter, we thought it might be useful to add one more example. The difference here is that this example is not from a school district but from a place in the business world. We thought that after all you have gone through, you might welcome something a little different yet something that supports our idea that the five characteristics of a successful leader work for all. Do not forget our initial definition that everyone who makes a decision that affects someone other than him or herself is a leader.

The business example is one that demonstrates the Theory Y individual to the max—giving very good feeling to the people involved—while still utilizing our five skills. This example takes place in sunny Florida and concerns a fairly large firm where management developed this good feeling to a science. The company, owned by one who could be considered a very perceptive and creative leader, believed that a satisfied employee is a productive employee.

The task, therefore, was to improve the quality and quantity of production while not alienating the staff. The group of insightful leaders looked at how employees operated and determined what might make their lives on the job a bit easier. By keeping in touch with the community—here meaning the workforce—they identified ideas that might increase morale and prove beneficial to the employees during the workday so as not to require employees to seek benefits off the clock! Being quite flexible, they decided to schedule a break in the workday where employees could unwind and use the company swimming pool.

Of course, bear in mind that with proper funding, you can do wonders to improve the overall work climate by giving employees, not only the resources to purchase supplies to do their job well, but also items that appear on their budget "wish" list. Unfortunately, our schools do not generally have such funds to engage in this type of activity.

You may recall that earlier in this book we mentioned the importance of rewarding staff. While we probably do not have it in our budgets to go out and build swimming pools, the lessons of the Professional Learning Communities state that a little reward goes a long way. Find ways that do fit your situation and show your staff that they are appreciated.

Therefore, as we outlined for you, the successful leader will learn how to use the proper skills to seek out resources and make optimum use of them while engaging the support of the entire community. The successful leader should direct his or her colleagues to the point where they are not asking, "What can my school district do for me?" but rather, "What can we do as a team to better our school or district?"

KEY POINTS

- As we address success stories for leaders of both education and the business world, we note the need to expand our resource pool. One place to start is the Internet by learning what other districts experienced and how they reached desirable goals as well as visiting the sites of such organizations as ThoughtBridge.
- The implementation of a system of rewards, no matter how seemingly small, will prove to be a great motivator and symbol of appreciation.

Chapter Eleven

One Final Point

Successful leadership will positively affect the lives of those you lead, reduce absenteeism, and foster good health of your staff. For example, we all know that good leadership creates a feeling in the environment of goodwill among its employees. That goodwill also encourages the sharing of lessons, ideas, and techniques. This kind of support helps the whole school in terms of raising the skills of the children. And, in the end, that is the goal that we all want.

A good climate encourages people to want to come to work, go the extra mile when it comes time for an unscheduled meeting, or react positively when asked to cover a class for a colleague who is absent because of an emergency. In other words, a good working environment and one in which the leader has earned the respect of his or her staff will facilitate the acceptance and implementation of new curriculum, instructional techniques, and organizational changes.

Consequently, incorrect implementation of any or all of the five characteristics of being a successful leader diminishes the efficiency of the company or school district by pulling the employee along unwillingly. The concept of Machiavellian successful leadership leads us to ponder his idea of relationships based on personal versus positional power. Machiavelli identified these powers as related to love (personal) or fear (position) and stated that it is better to be both feared and loved as long as fear does not lead to hatred.

We firmly and unequivocally believe and state, "Well, maybe!" But how do fear and love go together successfully? If leaders attempt to lean too much toward the Theory Y personality, it may appear that they are concerned more with winning the affection and admiration of their staff rather than trying to get the job done. Remember how Glueck and Ivancevich told us to mix the two? Too much of a good thing does not necessarily produce a good ending.

By the same token, no employees will give their best if they fear their employer. They will only do what they believe will not get them in trouble. That leaves out taking risks, experimentation to find new ways of accomplishing a goal, and possibly more efficient ways of doing the projects and tasks at hand. Fear may lead, as Machiavellian belief indicates, to hatred, and hatred may lead to retaliation, attempts to overthrow organizational goals, and the undermining of authority.

In terms of education, school board goals may be slowed by those who are in a position to carry out this kind of strategy. In addition, certain actions within the district or organization may be misinterpreted and therefore produce ill feelings, mistrust, and a result that was not the intended goal. If a person is made to feel afraid to add input that might go against the grain or has the potential of creating a disruption of events, progress is hindered as the intimidation continues.

This kind of ostrich-with-its-head-in-the-sand approach may result in a situation where those who have the least to lose are the only ones who are brave enough to take the lead. Without the input of the other staff members (those who fear their leaders), this type of behavior will result in the worst-case scenario. Generally, people with the least to lose do not possess the feeling of ownership we try to generate in our staff; therefore, they are the least likely to stand up for progress or to defend new initiatives.

An unsuccessful leader may use intimidation, fear, and negativity to motivate the employee. Leaders who practice this type of Theory X behavior leave out that ever-important trait of having strong, positive interpersonal skills. While this may produce ineffective actions, sometimes it works in getting some tasks completed. However, one has to wonder: Did the end justify the means? What does this kind of intimidation do to the employees? How is their commitment to excellence and the climate of the environment perceived? And finally, was the desired result really what their goal set out to accomplish in the long run?

A prime example of what can happen when a leader disregards the need to employ the five characteristics of a successful leader and instead fits the description of a true Theory X personality is illustrated in our story of the company cited in chapter 2. The adverse effects of this kind of leadership behavior influenced not only the personnel but also the organization as a whole. Our source at the company explained that the actions of this leader made them feel threatened to the point that they feared going to the manager with issues regarding work-related injuries or environmental concerns. They were led to believe that by going against the grain, their jobs would be in jeopardy and the workers would be further intimidated.

Before long, people were afraid to come to work but also afraid of being absent. There was a high level of anxiety and stress, low self-esteem, and a general feeling of not being appreciated. As a result, the negative impact on the employees, to the core of their beings, eventually led to a degradation of their health, and the bad feelings were subsequently carried home.

Employees who had a vested interest in the company were impacted more than others, as they believed that they were giving just that much more of themselves than more recently hired colleagues. People were afraid to make a lateral transfer within the company because they feared this would result in more consequences from the Theory X leader. They would save up their personal leave time and use it to search for employment outside of the organization. Some employees, who came from a good environment to this situation, discussed among themselves the lack of loyalty to the employer.

The direct correlation of this type of treatment and employee sentiment and productivity was that the workers did not care about the level of quality they put into their work. They did only enough to get by, and some people were so angered that they intentionally did poor-quality work but not enough to lose their jobs. They felt very vindictive and developed a sense of wanting to get back at management.

Chapter Twelve

Your Turn

We hope you found at least some of the information we provided useful for your personal situation. Now it is time to release you to take what you have gathered from this book and put it all into motion. Part of our research included a questionnaire that we circulated among administrators in different-sized school districts in different demographic areas. The questions we posed are offered here for your information and for your use.

You may want to keep them as is, or you may want to modify them to fit specific instances at your location. Perhaps at the next faculty or leadership meeting, you might wish to present this survey—or your modified version—to help you learn more about the people with whom you work and also to allow them to reflect on their roles in education. Circulate the survey for individual responses, or post them around a meeting area and have your staff or colleagues work in small groups to resolve the situations presented in each question.

If you choose the latter, a useful exercise would be to have the small groups come to their findings and then share with the entire audience either as a presentation or to open the floor for discussion. Again, you may use all our questions, select only those that are most relevant to your situation or to your group size, or create as many or as few needed for your group.

The situations posed here are hypothetical yet realistic as they apply to our daily routine. As you read each question, consider how one might employ each of the five characteristics when trying to address each situation. In doing so, you will first have to rank the characteristics in order of priority. Remember, while we want to try to use as many as possible, all situations do not require the same kind of attention; therefore, they may not require implementation of the same traits.

To help you along, we have listed the five characteristics at the end of each question. After the questionnaire, you will find an easy guide that summarizes the characteristics so that you will not have to keep referring back to the chapters.

Finally, we are including a rubric based in part on the theory of multiple intelligences as presented by Dr. Howard Gardner and Thomas Armstrong. We hope that this rubric will assist you in determining what type of leader you are so that you might better understand which of the five character traits you lean toward naturally and which you might have to work at a little.

1. A recent directive from your state department of education requires that all schools meet a specified level of student performance standards in order to continue to receive state funding. You are aware that a good percentage of your school or district will not be able to reach this goal in the time set by the state. You are also aware that budget constraints make it nearly impossible to begin special remediation programs such as after-school sessions designed to give extra attention to those students who, without such a program, are likely to score below the accepted performance standards.

                                              Order of Priority

A. Ability to be insightful   _____

B. Positive, strong interpersonal skills   _____

C. Self-growth   _____

D. Flexibility   _____

E. Keeping in touch with the community   _____

How are you going to assess the situation and rectify it in order to meet the state's requirements? How will you use the characteristics you believe are most crucial to get the job done?

2. You are a new administrator, and the overall school climate is one of mistrust. Last year, a teacher was denied tenure, and some staff members are concerned that you will follow the suit of previous administrators and not give them a chance to prove their worth.

                                              Order of Priority

A. Ability to be insightful   _____

B. Positive, strong interpersonal skills   _____

C. Self-growth   _____

D. Flexibility   _____

E. Keeping in touch with the community   _____

How do you begin the process of healing and building trust? Which characteristics will help you do so?

3. Your visions for the district, building, or department you lead differ greatly from those of your subordinates regarding education programs such as advanced placement, international baccalaureate, and honors. There is a strong voice from parents and the local business community—many companies whose futures rely heavily on graduates from your district—that leans toward dropping the program already in place in exchange for the program of their choice.

	Order of Priority
A. Ability to be insightful	_____
B. Positive, strong interpersonal skills	_____
C. Self-growth	_____
D. Flexibility	_____
E. Keeping in touch with the community	_____

What would be your course of action? How would you create an environment that is best suited for the students, community, and staff? Explain how to use these characteristics to your benefit.

4. You are introducing a new educational tool, such as curriculum mapping, to comply with the new state mandate for teaching math.

	Order of Priority
A. Ability to be insightful	_____
B. Positive, strong interpersonal skills	_____
C. Self-growth	_____
D. Flexibility	_____
E. Keeping in touch with the community	_____

How do you present this technique to a number of veteran teachers who are reluctant to change their established practices? Which characteristics will play a bigger role in helping you win the support of your staff?

5. You and your staff have been directed to formulate your own solutions to such issues as block scheduling, the safety of staff and students, and community concerns.

	Order of Priority
A. Ability to be insightful	_____
B. Positive, strong interpersonal skills	_____
C. Self-growth	_____
D. Flexibility	_____
E. Keeping in touch with the community	_____

How will you employ the five characteristics? Which will be the most important for your staff to use? How will you promote this positive behavior on their part?

6. Being professionally current is naturally important to being successful. Not keeping up with trends can be financially costly, cause stagnation among staff, and result in lowering student achievement.

	Order of Priority
A. Ability to be insightful	_____
B. Positive, strong interpersonal skills	_____
C. Self-growth	_____
D. Flexibility	_____
E. Keeping in touch with the community	_____

As an effective leader, how would you go about ensuring that you are on top of current trends? What skills might you use to lead others to pursue their own efforts of self-growth? How important is this characteristic in maintaining progress in your school or district? What are the implications if some faculty members do not pursue actions that promote self-growth?

7. Whether developing a budget, providing a positive environment, or creating a building "family" among your staff, you must model how a successful leader motivates and encourages an individual or group to take positive action.

	Order of Priority
A. Ability to be insightful	_____
B. Positive, strong interpersonal skills	_____
C. Self-growth	_____
D. Flexibility	_____
E. Keeping in touch with the community	_____

What attributes will empower you to model this behavior? How?

8. A new requirement for safety in schools that must be implemented by the end of the school year has been mandated. Budget issues become a major concern. You are in a crunch to meet the time line for implementation. An audit is scheduled for next month.

	Order of Priority
A. Ability to be insightful	_____
B. Positive, strong interpersonal skills	_____
C. Self-growth	_____
D. Flexibility	_____
E. Keeping in touch with the community	_____

What are the steps needed to set in motion the new requirements? How will you go about addressing the budget? Which of the characteristics will help you best?

9. Students started a prayer group after school. They have begun to hand out leaflets at the beginning of the day, during lunch, and in homerooms. Some parents and teachers are complaining that the distribution of these materials will be a major disruption to school procedures. Some students are threatening to hold a walkout to demonstrate their right to advertise their group.

	Order of Priority
A. Ability to be insightful	_____
B. Positive, strong interpersonal skills	_____
C. Self-growth	_____
D. Flexibility	_____
E. Keeping in touch with the community	_____

How will you diffuse the situation? What steps will you need to take? How will you encourage engagement of the characteristics by your staff and the parents?

10. Because of a sudden increase of theft of clothing in the school, the board of education has begun discussions to adopt a policy that requires students to wear school uniforms. Some students, parents, and community members support the policy, while others are strongly against such a strategy.

	Order of Priority
A. Ability to be insightful	_____
B. Positive, strong interpersonal skills	_____
C. Self-growth	_____
D. Flexibility	_____
E. Keeping in touch with the community	_____

How will you create a solution that will please both sides? What steps must be taken first? What programs or actions might work in this situation? Discuss how the characteristics will be helpful here.

11. You have just learned that the drastic change in demographics, partly due to new boundary definition, will have a major impact on your school this coming September. Many parents are demanding that you add new course selections. Staffing and the master schedule will be affected. Naturally, the budget will not increase at the same rate as the changes that must take place.

	Order of Priority
A. Ability to be insightful	_____
B. Positive, strong interpersonal skills	_____
C. Self-growth	_____
D. Flexibility	_____
E. Keeping in touch with the community	_____

How will you work with your staff and the community to ensure that your school maintains a high level of student performance? What role will each of the characteristics play in your planning?

12. Two teachers in your district or school building are in conflict over instructional techniques and classroom management. Instead of trying to work things out between them, their constant vocalization of these differences begins to affect the entire staff as people begin to take sides.

	Order of Priority
A. Ability to be insightful	_____
B. Positive, strong interpersonal skills	_____
C. Self-growth	_____
D. Flexibility	_____
E. Keeping in touch with the community	_____

Before this becomes a full-fledged civil war, what steps should be taken to calm the waters?

13. The teacher's union is trying to block the dismissal of a union employee deemed to be inefficient and insubordinate. As administrator for a particular department in what order of priority should the Essential Skills help you use to calm the waters after your teachers hear about the charge for dismissal.

	Order of Priority
A. Ability to be insightful	_____
B. Positive, strong interpersonal skills	_____
C. Self-growth	_____
D. Flexibility	_____
E. Keeping in touch with the community	_____

What kind of leader must you be in this situation before the union and your department teachers revolt by striking? What leadership skills would help you resolve this action?

14. Several states have initiated new requirements for teacher evaluations. Some are based on a point system involving classroom performance and standardized test scores. Others are based on whether a teacher is Exemplary, Proficient, Need Improvement, or Unsatisfactory. Other than legal action against a teacher what skills would you employ to persuade your staff that this is fair and a good measurement of a teacher's performance?

	Order of Priority
A. Ability to be insightful	_____
B. Positive, strong interpersonal skills	_____
C. Self-growth	_____
D. Flexibility	_____
E. Keeping in touch with the community	_____

To remind you what we have gone over thus far, next you will find the condensed version of the character traits of a successful leader. Refer to them as you answer the previous questions.

1. Ability to be insightful. An effective leader should be someone who can recognize future trends and their possible impact on current strategies. Knowledge of reform, new curricula, and constant challenges arising from global changes such as cultural and technological trends,

and the ability to work with these changes will provide for smooth and successful operations.
2. Positive, strong interpersonal skills. One should take the time to talk and listen to others. Sometimes it truly pays off to be a bit of the "guide on the side" rather than always being the "sage on the stage." A good rapport is essential so that others would actually enjoy working for or with you. Delegation of responsibilities brings new ideas to the table, gains the trust of coworkers, and reduces stress from the leader. For the good of the individual as well as the system as a whole, an effective leader should also encourage and support continued personal and professional development for staff members. Your coworkers and subordinates have diverse qualities, motivations, and personalities. An effective leader will be understanding and accepting of these differences.
3. Self-growth. In addition to ensuring that other staff members continue to shape their career paths, there are a wealth of seminars, classes, reading materials, and networks available for leaders at all levels that are generally easily accessible and as enjoyable as well as informative.
4. Flexibility. In our ever-changing society, the latest focus is on customer satisfaction. While this terminology was slow in its acceptance into the world of academia, it appears it is here to stay—at least for the foreseeable future. A successful leader must be resilient, be able to meet the current demand, and offer results that will appease the general public. In this case, the public can be defined as parents, other residents in the community, local businesses, universities, and the like.
5. Keeping in touch with the community. Successful politicians are in with the heartbeat of their constituents. Successful leaders in education must also be attuned to the needs of the community and maintain an ever-present yet always positive place in the community. This can be accomplished by attending not only Parent-Teacher-Student Association (PTSA) meetings but community-sponsored meetings as well. Planning and reviewing funding must include the entire community—business and general population growth, for example. An increase in a special section of the population, such as an influx in immigration or an increase of elderly residents could mean a need for a change in certain programs. Keeping in touch with the business community could be helpful in attaining support or funds through such actions as business partnership programs that might provide mentorship, technology donations to the school or district, support from large businesses for education programs such as broadcasting classes for high school students, or insight into the construction situation for both the community and the schools.

HOW TO SCORE THE SELF-ASSESSMENT

The survey in this chapter is not intended to determine where you place on a conventional scale. It was created so that you can gain a better idea of how you, as a leader, handle day-to-day situations. While reviewing your responses, you can draw a parallel between your actions and reactions and strengths as they relate to the theory of multiple intelligences (MI). While the MI theory is not an exact science and is very much open to interpretation, one can say that, based on the frequency of your selection of character traits employed for each survey question, you tend to lean toward one or more of the multiple intelligences.

However, you must keep in mind that the intelligences are not mutually exclusive. An MI profile will vary, depending on personal growth and changes as well as particular situations. Therefore, you will better understand how you might respond to similar issues. Additionally, you will be able to identify the MI preferences of your staff and colleagues and use this information to create a harmonious and successful working atmosphere. We offer here an umbrella of the MI categories as:

- Logical/mathematical
- Interpersonal
- Intrapersonal
- Verbal/linguistic

If you chose "ability to be insightful" as your most frequent response, you tend to be a logical/mathematical leader. The logical/mathematical leader has the ability to assess a situation and, with relative speed, compare the issues with past experiences, analyze the data, and move forward in a positive and successful manner.

If you chose "flexibility" or "positive, strong interpersonal skills" as your most frequent response, you tend to be an interpersonal, social leader. You might be the one in your school or district who initiates actions or calls together representatives from several groups for a problem-solving session. In addition, good interpersonal skills will help develop a sense of trust, which builds toward an open and democratic workplace. Fear of retribution for new ideas and concerns that are not compatible with the leader will fade away.

If you chose "self-growth" as your most frequent response, you tend to be an intrapersonal leader. You tend to seek opportunities that enhance your ability to assess and solve simple and complex situations. For example, given the rapid pace of change in our environment, it is often difficult to find college courses that address these issues. Workshops and conferences do appear on a timelier basis, and you are apt to search for these venues, attend them, and report your findings back to your school or district.

If you chose "keeping in touch with the community" as your most frequent response, you tend to be a verbal/ linguistic leader. Your strongest skills lay in your ability to work with your staff, PTSA, school board, and other components of the community in order to remain current with the trends in education and needs of the community.

Bibliography

Argyris, C. (2000). *Flawed Advice and the Management Trap: How Managers Can Know When They're Getting Good Advice and When They're Not.* New York: Oxford University Press.

Armstrong, T. (1993). *7 Kinds of Smart: Identifying and Developing Your Multiple Intelligences.* New York: Plume.

Bagin, D., Gallagher, D. R., & Kindred, L. W. (1994). *The School and Community Relations.* Boston: Allyn and Bacon.

Blanchard, K., & Hersey, P. (1982). *Management of Organizational Behavior: Utilizing Human Resources.* Englewood Cliffs, NJ: Prentice Hall.

Borum, R., Fein, R. A., Modzeleski, W., Pollack, W. S., Reddy, M., & Vossekuil, B. (2002). *Threat Assessment in Schools: A Guide to Managing Threatening Situations and to Creating Safe School Climates.* Washington, DC: U.S. Secret Service and U.S. Department of Education.

Borum, R., Fein, R. A., Modzeleski, W., Reddy, M., & Vossekuil, B. (2002). *The Final Reports and Findings of the Safe School Initiative for the Prevention of School Attacks in the United States.* Washington, DC: U.S. Secret Service and U.S. Department of Education.

Clarke, J., Bossange, J., Erb, C., Gibson, D., Nelligan, B., Spencer, C., & Sullivan, M. (2000). *Dynamics of Change.* Providence, RI: Brown University.

DuFour, R., & Eaker, R. (1998). *Professional Learning Communities at Work.* Bloomington, IN: National Education Service.

Fullan, M. (2001). *Leading in a Culture of Change.* San Francisco: Jossey-Bass.

Ivancevich, J., & Glueck, W. F. (1983). *Foundations of Personnel: Human Resource Management.* Plano, TX: Business Publications, Inc.

Jacobs, M. M., & Langley, N. (2002). "Profiles in Leadership." *American School Board Journal* 189: 64–68.

Milken Family Foundation and the National Association of Secondary School Principals. (November 2001). "Priorities and Barriers in High School Leadership: A Survey of Principals." Reston, VA: NASSP.

Paterson, J. (1997). *Coming Clean about Organizational Change— Leadership in the Real World.* Arlington, VA: American Association of School Administrators.

Scarnati, J. (2002). "The Godfather Theory of Management: An Exercise in Power and Control." *Management Decisions* 40, no. 9: 834–41.

WEBSITES

While conducting our research, we found the following websites useful. We list them here for your convenience. However, as we often find, many websites are not always kept current or are deleted over time. Keeping that in mind, we limited our list to those that are from government organizations or other such sources that are likely to be around for quite some time.

http://www.cgcs.org/reports/foundations.html. The site illustrates a study titled "Case Studies of How Urban School Systems Improve Student Achievement" and discusses the implications regarding leadership effectiveness in urban school systems.

http://www.cis.org.

http://www.ed.gov/nclb/overview/intro/execsumm.html. This site, sponsored by the U.S. Department of Education, has several pertinent topics relevant for today. For example, you will find information and articles on the No Child Left Behind Act as relates to students, parents, and administrators.

http://www.fbi.gov/about-us/cjis/ucr/nibrs/crime-in-schools-and-colleges-pdf.

http://www.fbi.gov/stats-services/crimestats.

http://www.fbi.gov/stats-services/publications/2011-national-gang-threat-assessment. This official Federal Bureau of Investigation site offers news and statistical information about a variety of crime information.

http://www.fcps.edu. A website to one of the largest school districts in the country, this site offers information on the PALS program cited in this text as well as samples of successful programs for the entire school community.

http://www.learningfirst.org/best-leaders-neediest-schools. This site provides a place for educators and parents to share and learn about current policy, trends, and overall professional growth opportunities. It is a good site to visit to find out what schools across the country are doing and how to benefit from their success.

http://www.thomasarmstrong.com/multiple-intelligences.html. Thomas Armstrong offers insight to Dr. Howard Gardner's theory of multiple intelligences, a self-growth tool to help leaders understand their strengths and potential.

http://www.teacherspayteachers.com. A site where educators can share ideas and lesson plans. There is also an extensive offer of every type of consumable items—written, recorded, Common Core textbooks, etc.—for educators to purchase at extremely affordable prices.

www.thoughtbridge.net. Leaders looking for an alternative method of resolving conflicts between clients will find this website useful.

http://www.washingtonpost.com/blogs/answer-sheet/post/why-states-should-refuse-duncans-nclb-waivers/2011/08/08/gIQAhKJQ3I_blog.html. This site takes you directly to the articles related to No Child Left Behind in the largest newspaper in Washington, D.C.: the *Washington Post*

About the Authors

Nancy Langley, MEd, has been a world languages teacher, team leader, and department chair in secondary schools in Northern Virginia. **Mark M. Jacobs**, EdD, has more than thirty years of experience as an administrator and teacher at elementary schools, secondary schools, and college. Both are active in professional development workshops and conferences for educators of all levels. Together they have conducted extensive research on educational leadership. Their efforts resulted in an article published by the *American School Board Journal* in September 2002: "Profiles in Leadership" as well as subsequent lectures and workshops at venues such as the School Administrators Association of New York State Conference in New York; the American Association of School Administrators in New Orleans; Fairfax County Public Schools in-service in Oakton, Virginia; and the Northeast Conference for Teachers of Foreign Language in New York City.

www.ingramcontent.com/pod-product-compliance
Lightning Source LLC
Chambersburg PA
CBHW070337230426
43663CB00011B/2356